praise for
BRAD HERZOG

"Herzog's books are emerging as the new classics of American travel writing." —*American Book Review*

"A terrifically capable writer, styled with a dash of Paul Theroux and a dollop of Tom Wolfe... Herzog's prose is facile and satisfying, oftentimes stunning... There is plenty of time for a history lesson, an absorbing anecdote, or a thought-provoking detour." —*Ithaca Times*

"This man knows how to do road trips. He's a Picasso of the Winnebago." —*Orlando Sentinel*

DETOUR

2020

a cross-country drive through america's wrong turns

Brad Herzog

Better days ahead!

Why Not Books
Pacific Grove, California

WHY NOT BOOKS

www.WhyNotBooks.com

info@WhyNotBooks.com

ISBN: 978-0-9978808-8-5

Cover and interior design and layout by Tessa Avila

TO TALMA AND MICHAEL
for generously providing the house on wheels

AND TO STEPH AND ADAM
for graciously providing the home away from home

Contents

DETOUR

2020

N ew Hope is somewhere, but I don't see the signs.
The map tells me it's an unincorporated community
along this stretch of Route 5 in southern Virginia, but it looks
to be little more than a couple of gas pumps and a country store.
Unmarked. Blink and you miss it. I'm only 30 miles into a 3,400-
mile journey, and already my roadmap is shrugging. Summer is
waning as I make my way westward. Autumn will soon arrive—
reluctantly, I assume, with a deep breath and a hard swallow, like
a bearer of bad tidings preparing to face an angry crowd.

This is 2020, after all.

Already it has muscled its way onto everyone's list of one of
the most god-awful years in American history. The worst global
health crisis since 1918. More Americans out of work than in the
Great Depression. Unimaginable wildfires scorching the West
and creating hellish skyscapes across the country. Social unrest
echoing the chaos and cultural confrontations of 1968, and civil
discourse in shambles. A government so cruel and incompetent
that it separates children from their parents at the border and
loses track of mom and dad. A nation so polarized that fears of a new
civil war have moved from hyperbole to the realm of possibility.

We've all talked about it, so much so that the notion has become cliché long before the year is even over. The memes proliferate: Doc from *Back to the Future* warns Marty, "Whatever you do, don't go to 2020." A knight, armored head to toe, still receives an arrow through his eye slit. A question: If 2020 were a drink, what would it be? Answer: Colonoscopy prep.

The peripheral news has started to seem absurdly apocalyptic, almost sardonic:

**DEATH VALLEY SOARS TO 130 DEGREES,
POTENTIALLY EARTH'S HIGHEST TEMPERATURE**

**INTENSIFYING HURRICANES ARE HELPING
INVASIVE SPECIES SPREAD ACROSS THE U.S.**

**TEXAS GOVERNOR ISSUES DISASTER DECLARATION
OVER BRAIN-EATING AMOEBA**

When we hear about murder hornets in Washington or zombie cicadas in West Virginia or giant Saharan dust storms or sun-blotting plagues of locusts in Kenya or gangs of monkeys taking over the streets of Thailand, the default response these days is a shake of the head, a wry chuckle, and simply "That's so 2020." We watch a football game. The announcer discusses injuries: "Everyone's hurt. It's 2020, for crying out loud." And even when we can perceive some positives—say, an electorate motivated to vote as never before—we wake up the next morning to a headline like this:

**ASTEROID HEADING OUR WAY
RIGHT BEFORE ELECTION DAY**

Amid these converging calamities, we're doing our best to greet each day with resolve and make the most of a forced paradigm shift. But we're weary and wary, tired of most every decision requiring existential considerations and fearful of what might happen next. We're discombobulated, divorced from our routine, missing our families and friends, shaken by the loss of control over our lives. Meanwhile, an aspiring autocrat in a MAGA hat abdicates leadership, amplifying COVID denials while cases surge. He brazenly games the electoral system in advance of the most important election in modern U.S. history, as he prepares to gaslight victory and won't promise a peaceful transfer of power if the results don't satisfy him. As he dismantles democracy in plain sight, the sense of impending doom that has hovered over a huge swath of the population for years now has seemed to peak.

Hopefully.

We are at an American inflection point. We all feel it. So I'm taking a drive.

My goal is to chronicle this unprecedented moment—this "season of darkness," as Joe Biden described it—amid this unfathomable year. Not 2020 in hindsight, but in real time. Not from a lonely writing room, but through an expedition into the heart of America and its conflicts, its history, its tragic deviations. By the time this is documented, the nation may have tipped toward one direction or the other. Or its future may still hang in the balance. But this particular moment requires recording—one mile marker at a time—if only to assess where we are.

This is a spontaneous undertaking, primarily motivated by the simple fact that I have to get home and by the appeal of turning an obligatory journey into a meandering exploration. As the song goes, I'm going to California with an aching in my heart. After spending the summer with my family in Wisconsin, I dropped off my son in Williamsburg, Virginia, where he and three friends randomly landed following a summer-long house search. They've opted for a COVID pause from campus life, among the millions worldwide whose best-laid plans have been crumpled and tossed. I don't know when I'll see my firstborn again. It is ironic, I suppose, that he finds himself just a few blocks from the living history museum of Colonial Williamsburg—in fact, sharing the property with a professional blacksmith who trudges to an 18th-century armory every day in period costume. As I make my way home, my son will be immersing himself in a nation's beginnings, while I'll be exploring its possible demise.

We had momentum, of course. We had elected the first Black president. It looked certain that the first woman would follow him into the Oval Office, a development well past due. The economy had fully recovered from a monumental recession. We were addressing climate change through an international accord and were en route to making green energy an economic opportunity. It seemed like we were continuing the progressive climb toward enlightenment in America. Our path was clear, our engine sound, and the road seemed to rise to meet us.

And then the momentum stopped. Sputtered. Died.

So it turns out that I'm driving a metaphor home. To make our way safely out to the Midwest, my family had borrowed a little camper from a generous friend back in our hometown. "Take it for the summer," she said, while she sheltered in place. The RV had accrued some 145,000 miles over the years, but a pre-trip inspection had given us the greenlight. And it was all green lights—until the alternator conked out in eastern Montana, in a place so middle-of-nowhere that the closest reference point was the location of the Battle of Little Bighorn.

Following an afternoon of angst, a long backtrack toward civilization, and a hefty bill, we were back on our way. But before we could complete our drive through North Dakota, the "check engine" light came on, and every time I would coast to a stop the damn thing would cough and surge and gasp and go silent. It has been happening ever since. By now, mechanics in four states have tried to diagnose the problem. A new throttle connector. No, a burned-out spark plug and wire. Uh-uh, it obviously needs a new idle air control valve. And each time, the RV seems fine for a day—until it isn't. I've forked over fourteen hundred bucks, and still the same problem: Stop. Surge. Sputter. Stall.

And I have more than three thousand miles ahead of me.

Thus, a love-hate relationship with my little COVID-cautious bubble on wheels, which allows me the luxury of exploration but adds yet another layer of stress to my world. I figure this enigmatic vehicle deserves a name. "Rocinante" would have been perfect. Like my camper, Don Quixote's horse was an old nag past its prime, aspiring to legendary feats but overmatched. Unfortunately, John Steinbeck borrowed the name for his travels exactly 60 years ago. So I seek a sobriquet that captures the zeitgeist of this rotten year—the confusion, the exasperation, the crises exacerbated by a petty president's tweeted id, and the sense that the nation's pilot has fallen asleep at the wheel.

My choice is obvious. I'll call it Covfefe. One man's gibberish is another man's deliverance.

If you're hoping for a dispassionate assessment of America, hitch a ride with someone else. This drive will be fueled by too much unleaded gas and no shortage of opinions, few of them likely to be seen through a rose-colored windshield. After all, you can't drive cross-country in neutral.

And everywhere I go, mile by mile, town by town, I'll be trying to answer much the same question: How the hell did we get here?

ANGELA

launch my muse across America just down the road from Williamsburg—at the beginning. Not the Jamestown that I learned about in elementary school: John Smith, John Rolfe, Pocahontas, a nation's origin story. Rather, I'm focused on the Jamestown tale that wasn't taught: The story of Angela and a nation's original sin.

So the narrative actually begins some seven thousand miles away—on a lush, green plateau 150 miles from the Atlantic Ocean. The young woman, perhaps in her mid-thirties, was a citizen of the Ndongo Kingdom, one of the most influential kingdoms in West Central Africa, in what is now Angola. Since the mid-1400s, Ndongo had been trading with the kings and queens of Portugal, but by 1617 the relationship had soured, mostly because the Portuguese began pillaging resources from Ndongo. Including people. The colonial power enlisted a feared tribal adversary to round up thousands of men, women, and children 130 miles east of Portugal's coastal Luanda colony. In fact, about 50,000 slaves were exported from Angola over only a four-year span. Angela was among them.

She was marched more than 70 miles to a Portuguese fort along the Kwanza River where she was bathed, baptized, branded, then sold and rowed to a slave ship anchored in the harbor. There were 350 enslaved Africans aboard the *San Juan Bautista* in early summer 1619; after being chained and packed amid the filth in the hold of the ship, barely half of them arrived alive in Veracruz, on Mexico's coast. In August, the *San Juan Bautista* was attacked off that coast by a pair of British privateers. Most of the captives were taken aboard the *White Lion,* which eventually made its way to Virginia, where "20 and odd Negroes" were sold in exchange for food. Angela was taken aboard the *Treasurer* and arrived four days later. Three colonists were dispatched to meet the ship, including a tobacco farmer and merchant named William Pierce.

Pierce's wife and daughter had arrived in Jamestown in 1609, but he had boarded a different ship, which was fated to encounter a hurricane and wash ashore in Bermuda. By the time Pierce and his cohorts constructed a new ship and reached Jamestown, they encountered only 60 gaunt survivors (including Pierce's family) of a horrific winter that had caused roughly three-quarters of the English colonists to perish. The Starving Time.

"The settlers were forced to eat rats, snakes, cats, dogs, horses, shoe leather. They even resorted to cannibalism," says the young tour guide to a socially distanced, half-masked crowd beneath the Tercentennial Monument, erected on the 300th anniversary of the what the inscription says is "the birthplace of Virginia and the United States." And then the woman adds, epically understated, "So they weren't doing so great." I steal a glance toward a nearby bench occupied by a man in a "Keep America Great" hat. I figure he hasn't grasped the irony.

Thirty-two Africans were counted in a census that year and described as "in ye service of several planters." A few years later, one of them, living in the household of William Pierce, was listed in the colony muster with the Portuguese spelling of the Christian name she had been given: "Angelo, a Negro Woman." Much is known about Pierce, but it is only in the last few years that the Jamestown Rediscovery Foundation excavated the property—an area now known as the Angela Site. In a search for more information about the first African woman on Jamestown Island for whom there is a name and at least part of a story, they removed hundreds of years of soil, one layer at a time.

And oh the layers. By mid-century, there were about 300 slaves in the Virginia Colony. By the end of the century, as tobacco farmers became dependent on slave labor, the number of people there who were African or of African descent totalled more than 16,000. There is historical confusion about how many were slaves (a word not even in the legal lexicon at the time) and how many were indentured servants who could eventually gain their freedom. But in 1640, a Black man named John Punch and two white servants (a Dutchman and a Scot) ran away from their Virginia employer. After they were apprehended in Maryland, the two white runaways were punished with extended terms of service, but Punch was made a "servant for life." It was the beginning of a legal process that soon would equate near-universal bondage with people of African descent. A couple of decades later, a statute declared that any child born to an enslaved mother would be considered enslaved, too. Soon, Black residents of Jamestown were restricted from owning livestock and from trial by jury for capital crimes. The area's power brokers were closing legal loopholes. No more ambiguities. African slavery was entrenched and codified. If the arrival of the first slave ship was the moment when, as Langston Hughes put it, "freedom stumped its toe" at Jamestown, now freedom was amputated at the ankle.

Over the next century and a half following Angela's arrival, nearly 400 vessels brought kidnapped Africans to Virginia. By the time of the Civil War, an estimated 10 million people of African descent had been enslaved in America. All the tragedies and triumphs that followed—in a Tuskegee laboratory, on a Montgomery bus, at a Topeka elementary school and a Little Rock high school, at a Greensboro lunch counter, in a Birmingham church, over a Selma bridge, along a Mississippi dirt road and the streets of Tulsa and the Lower Ninth Ward of New Orleans, in a Washington Heights ballroom, on a Memphis balcony, on the side of an L.A. freeway, on a football sideline in San Francisco, outside a grocery store in Minneapolis, even a million strong on the National Mall in January 2008... all of it started with Angela and those "20 and odd Negroes" brought to Jamestown.

In 2020, four hundred years after Angela, the median wealth of Black households is roughly one-tenth that of white households. In 2020, four centuries on, Black men are 2.5 times more likely than white men to be killed by police. In 2020, some sixteen generations later, the coarseness of history has led to tens of thousands of protesters shouting a three-word mantra that is saddening in its obviousness. The retort—by people who insist they're not racist, merely realist—is that "all lives matter." Which, let's face it, is just a notch above "whatever."

I stand there, alone with my thoughts. The archaeologists have moved on to another section of land, closer to the river. Most of the handful of visitors are gathering around Jamestown's original church and fort a few hundred yards away. The Angela Site sits quietly, a story still left largely undiscovered. Now a family of four approaches. They glance at the sign showing Angela's mention in the 1624 "Muster of Captain William Pierce." They look over at the ruins for a few moments before the dad tugs on their dog's leash and the mom separates the kids, and they move on without comment or discussion.

It can be hard to impart history. But I am encouraged that Historic Jamestown is trying, telling not the history I learned as a suburban kid in the '70s. They no longer whitewash the profoundly imperfect aspects of America's first permanent settlement. There is an occasional First Africans Walking Tour. Guides will point to a spot where the first legislative assembly in the Western Hemisphere convened. "Freedom over there." Then they'll point to the Angela Site and say, "Slavery over here." Signposts pull no punches. One explains how "not all Virginians were represented" by Jamestown's first General Assembly. Not women. Not the natives. Not indentured servants. Not slaves. Another reveals the words of the Virginia Slave Code of 1705: "All servants imported and brought into the Country... who were not Christians in their native country... shall be accounted and be slaves... All Negro, mulatto and Indian slaves within this dominion... shall be held to be real estate."

In fact, a year ago, before COVID-19—before the state of the nation went from horrible to horrific—a costumed interpreter used to reenact Angela's story as best she could. Wearing a gray shirt, soiled apron and yellow head wrap, she would stand along the windswept banks of the James River and tell a crowd about her tale of pain and suffering, of freedom in Angola and bondage in a strange land. "Every day I rise," she would say, "and I come to a place and I cry."

Given that there are so few accounts of enslaved people in the public record, so many millions whose namelessness prevents African Americans from knowing their ancestry, Angela has been called "a symbolic holy mother for generations." When a visitor once asked the costumed interpreter why the story of this enslaved woman was never part of his colonial history lessons, she replied, "What if now is the time we are supposed to know about Angela?"

Never mind what Angela herself might think about such a portrayal, the point is that Historic Jamestown isn't hiding a nascent nation's true nature. Its interpreters and archaeologists are attempting to fill in the blanks of American history, warts and all. And yes, it is part of a movement to reframe history as truth-telling rather than what it largely has been for hundreds of years—stories told from the historical perspective of those in power. The movement recognizes that not only were the so-called protagonists of our history flawed, but the telling of that history has been flawed, too.

The most newsworthy manifestation of this has been the 1619 Project, developed by *The New York Times Magazine* as a collection of articles, poems, short fiction, photo essays, podcasts, and finally educational resources and curricula for teachers to use. The Project's ambitious goal: "reframe the country's history by placing the consequences of slavery and the contributions of Black Americans at the very center of the national narrative." The Project originated with a special magazine issue that aimed to portray how the various branches of systemic inequality have their roots in slavery. The essays had titles like "America Wasn't a Democracy Until Black Americans Made It One" and "Why Doesn't America Have Universal Healthcare? One Word: Race" and "Why Is Everyone Always Stealing Black Music?"

The telling of history impacts the understanding of contemporary society, which influences the course of the future. Reasonable people can disagree about the degree to which the narrative is recast. But how can any person of conscience begrudge a movement, based on motivated inclusiveness, that attempts to validate the experiences of the long disenfranchised? How can anyone with any understanding of historical complexities and the spectrum of humanity possibly cast the need for a more multicultural perspective of history as something sinister?

Cue Donald Trump. The man puts the obvious in oblivious. Predictably, he opted to go to battle. To celebrate Independence Day in 2020, he gave a stupendously self-aggrandizing speech in front of Mount Rushmore (his people would later inquire about adding him to the monument, which is a bit like making Charles Manson the fifth Beatle). "Our children," he oozed, "are taught in school to hate their own country and to believe that the men and women who built it were not heroes, but were villains."

When FOX's Chris Wallace later asked him where that notion came from, Trump answered, "I just look at—I look at schools. I watch, I read, look at the stuff. Now they want to change—1492, Columbus discovered America. You know, we grew up, you grew up, we all did, that's what we learned. Now they want to make it the 1619 Project. Where did that come from? What does it represent? I don't even know, so..."

"It's slavery," said Wallace.

"That's what they're saying, but they don't even know. They just want to make a change."

This wasn't a learned scholar suggesting that perhaps 1619 is a somewhat arbitrary date because tens of thousands of African men and women already had been transported across the Atlantic against their will on Spanish ships, or that the focus on "settlers" and slaves might relegate the plight of displaced Native Americans to secondary consideration, or even that the sincere attempt to investigate the historical impact of racial injustice might occasionally have veered into cynical interpretations of that history. Can you even imagine Trump summoning such intellectual nuance?

No, this was a willfully ignorant *president of the United States* refusing to even acknowledge the legitimacy of accepted history or the power of learning from it. Trumpeting his historical myopia. Dismissing, with a wave of his hand, any pretext to understanding the origins of the country that he is supposed to steward. Promoting instead an executive order to teach "patriotic education"—a terrifying phrase—through an effort called the 1776 Commission, Trump said the 1619 Project has been "totally discredited." Yes, by a man who talked of Frederick Douglass in the present tense and ad-libbed a bit about airports being attacked during the Revolutionary War.

Just a couple of days after he banned federal agencies from conducting racial sensitivity training that he deemed "un-American propaganda," he tweeted that the Department of Education is looking into whether California schools have included the 1619 Project in their curriculums. "If so, they will not be funded!" Consider that for a moment: He threatened to defund public schools if they don't teach history to his liking. GOP Senator Tom Cotton even introduced legislation aimed at codifying this. He called it the Saving American History Act of 2020. Sigh. Let's start by saving America from privilege-preserving propagandists.

But naturally, the battle rages. Between those who want to broaden the scope of history and those who claim it is being wholly rewritten. Between those who want to mine deeper into the truth and those who want to preserve the self-serving and blindly celebratory layer of legend on top, as if history's only purpose is to make the young and privileged feel good about their ancestry. So this is one of the many precipices on which we stand—a nation that needs fixing, but a faction that refuses to learn from its mistakes by even acknowledging them.

Nobody knows what happened to Angela in the years that followed her arrival on Jamestown Island. Did she bear children? Live past middle age? Was she sent elsewhere? Did she ever regain her freedom? Her fate remains unknown, but she has a name. More than that, she has a *presence*.

Last year, amid their layer by layer excavation, the archaeological team at the Angela Site made a simple but thrilling discovery. One of the staff archaeologists at the time was a young woman named—and here fate came to play—Angelina. She grew up obsessed with America's origins. Forget Disney World. As a child in New Jersey, she would beg her mom to take her to Jamestown. So after graduating from Washington College, Angelina Towery-Tomasura joined a Jamestown team that kept an artist's rendering of Angela in its shed, a reminder that their mission was personal.

Over a few years of digging, layer by layer in 100-square-foot segments, the crew typically found mundane artifacts—broken bricks, pieces of roofing slate, countless square-headed nails from colonial smiths. Once in a while, a European-made ceramic dish that might have been handled by a servant. Or a pipe bowl, or an amber bottle. But on this day in 2019, exactly four centuries after Angela's arrival, they uncovered four shells—oval, dime-sized, with jagged teeth on either side of the opening down the center. Cowrie shells from the Indian Ocean. In Africa, they were used as currency and considered a symbol of fertility. Someone had added small holes to the shells, opened at the back. They might have been jewelry, perhaps Angela's only tangible attachment to her home. Angie, the archaeologist, remembers that her crew was quiet for much of the rest of the day. Her explanation of their quest: "Her story is written in the dirt. We are driven to find it. We want to give Angela a voice." To borrow a current phrase not unrelated to her story, Angela's life matters.

I take one last look at the James River—perhaps Angela's last view, too—and climb back into Covfefe. It's hot. The engine sputters, surges, coughs, dies. I have a whole continent to cross. When I finally rev the RV to life and head west—"always west," as Ken Kesey once put it—I turn to a randomized iTunes song list. That's when I have a movie moment. In *Adventures in the Screen Trade*, screenwriter William Goldman described how he was once driving with someone who said, "I wonder what the weather's going to be tomorrow." He flicked on the radio and instantly heard something like, "Tomorrow's weather calls for heavy rains..." It is a moment that happened, but would be implausible on the big screen. Or as Goldman wrote in *The Princess Bride*, "Inconceivable."

So this was my movie moment to launch my journey: As I'm driving away from the Angela Site, my head swimming in thoughts of a brave woman's ordeal and the centuries of struggle that have followed, an Englishman croons in my ears. Mick Jagger.

Angie, Angie
When will those clouds all disappear?
Angie, Angie
Where will it lead us from here?

THE WAR BETWEEN
THE STATES OF MIND
APPOMATTOX, VIRGINIA

For much of the day, I have been accompanied by a reluctant rain, as if the clouds can't seem to strike a compromise. More than a drizzle, not quite a downpour. A sky dimmed, but not quite darkened. Certainly not blue. Quite a bit of a gray.

Perfect, really. Because much of the drive here feels—how do I put this?—convincingly Confederate. Maybe it's the Dixie Dream Ice Cream shop in the town of Cumberland. Or the geographical hiccups that smell somehow southern-fried to me: Troublesome Creek. Ducks Corner. Gobbler Hill. Old Grist Mill Road. Or the semi-barricaded Robert E. Lee Wayside, where I stop anyway and listen to the rain metronome against Covfefe's tin roof and where a rusting sign informs me that "just to the south" a monument marks where Lee pitched his tent on the night of April 12-13, 1865, before he surrendered to Ulysses Grant. And there's that series of antebellum plantations radiating from Williamsburg along Highway 5. Westover Plantation. Berkeley Plantation. Shirley Plantation. Sherwood Forest Plantation.

What's the difference between a farm and a plantation? The answer has something to do with subsistence farming versus cash crops. Tobacco. Sugar cane. Cotton. And in the South, of course, that meant forced labor. So that word... it's a loaded one. When it first appeared in English, "plantation" had two broad meanings—establishment of an institution, and the planting of seeds in the ground. Now the word is inseparable from the institution of slavery. It's not that I believe these places shouldn't be called plantations. I think we should confront history instead of pretending it isn't there. But certainly, we shouldn't be bolstering the plantation myth—the nauseating notion that the relationship between masters and slaves was not about bondage, but some sort of benevolence. The myth was perpetuated by plantation novels like *Gone with the Wind*—you know, the book that became Donald Trump's professed favorite movie. He said so to a drooling crowd while criticizing selection of the film *Parasite* as an Oscar-winner: "And the winner was a movie from... South Korea. What the hell was that all about?... Let's get *Gone with the Wind*. Can we get *Gone with the Wind* back, please?" Because that is what presidents should care about, right? Just as COVID-19 was reaching our shores. What good is xenophobic nationalism without a dash of nostalgic racism?

I digress, but while I'm on the subject...

If ever a place was in need of a name change, it's Highway 5, which honors a Virginia native, 10th U.S. President John Tyler. Frankly, the Steven Tyler Memorial Highway would be less inappropriate. Tyler was the first vice president elevated to the top spot when his predecessor died. But if you spotted me the "T," gave me four more letters to work with and told me a bit about the man, I'd fill out "TRUMP" in the crossword puzzle. To wit:

- Never truly figured he'd be president. (The Whigs added him to the ticket on a whim. In the famous campaign slogan—"Tippecanoe and Tyler, too!"—he was the afterthought.)
- Startlingly ill-informed. (When William Henry Harrison keeled over just a month after taking office, Tyler hadn't even known the president was ill.)
- Mocked, justifiably, for being in over his head. (His rivals called him "His Accidency.")
- Anathema to many in his party. (The Whigs expelled him.)
- Treated his cabinet like a season of *The Apprentice*. (All but one member resigned.)
- Had an authoritarian streak. (Tyler: "I can never consent to being dictated to as to what I shall or shall not do.")
- Went all-in on the wrong side of moral history. (He was a lifelong slaveholder who advocated for states' rights and ignored the pursuit of equal justice.)
- Treasonous. (After he left office, he was elected to the Confederate Congress.)
- Had multiple wives. (His first wife bore him eight children).
- Remarried to a woman a generation younger than he. (He had seven more children with her, the last arriving when Tyler was 70.)

One of those children fathered children of his own when he was in *his* seventies, a couple of whom are *still alive* (in their nineties) as I embark on this journey. So here is possibly my favorite nugget of trivia ever: John Tyler was born during George Washington's presidency, delivered Thomas Jefferson's funeral address, and served in the Oval Office two decades before Abraham Lincoln. Yet two of his *grandchildren*—just two generations removed from a slave-owning president—lived to see the first Black commander-in-chief. I'm not sure how the grandkids felt, but I'm certain Grandpa rolled over in his grave. He would have liked Trump, though.

The lesson is clear, and it drives my journey: American history is not yet ancient history. Worse yet, America feels on the verge of repeating its most disastrous historical mistakes.

As I pass one of those old plantations—2,500-acre Evelynton Farm, still family-owned and operated—I can almost smell the stench emanating from the family's patriarch, a colossal jackass named Edmund Ruffin. He even looked the part. Straight white hair down to his shoulders. Cruel eyes. He could have passed for a fire-breathing preacher. Ruffin was born into aristocracy and inherited a fortune, owning several plantations and nearly 100 slaves. He was rabidly pro-slavery and an instigator of the lowest order. There are modern parallels. Obvious ones.

Ruffin—described by at least one historian as "deranged" and "maniacal"—aligned himself with the Fire-Eaters, a group of secessionist agitators whose shameless rhetoric was designed to weaken a nation's already fragile unity. As sectional hostilities increased, he didn't pull back from his bombast. He amplified it. Sound familiar?

In 1859, after abolitionist John Brown was captured following an attempted slave revolt at Harper's Ferry, Ruffin found a way to revel in revenge. Then in his mid-sixties, he actually joined the Virginia Military Institute corps of cadets and traveled hundreds of miles, weapon in hand, solely to observe the man's execution. Brown had intended to arm slaves with pikes, many of which were captured from him. Ruffin purchased several and sent one to each governor of the slave-holding states as a symbol of meeting progressive aggression with dominance. "You have to dominate, if you don't dominate, you're wasting your time." Ruffin didn't say that; Trump did during a phone call with governors about responding to urban rioting after the murder of George Floyd.

In 1860, Ruffin published a book written in the form of letters from a fictional English resident, sort of the way Trump used to pose as a public relations man to promote himself to the tabloids. In the book, Ruffin imagined the aftermath of that year's presidential election. He had hoped that William Seward would win the Republican nomination because he considered him his most targetable foil—just like Trump hoped Bernie Sanders would take the Democratic primary. When Lincoln got the nod, Ruffin wasn't sure what to do with a presidential candidate hell-bent on uniting the nation. So he doubled down on his divisiveness. "He will destroy this country... demolish our cherished destiny... give free reign to violent anarchists... they do not see America as the most free, just and exceptional nation on earth. Instead, they see a wicked nation that must be punished for its sins."

That wasn't Ruffin either. That was Trump, about Joe Biden.

Ruffin's book predicted the Civil War, even forecasting that it would start with a southern attack on Fort Sumter in South Carolina. But this didn't turn out to be passive commentary—because it turns out that Ruffin actually fired one of the first shots. After Lincoln's election he traveled to South Carolina to encourage disunion, even sailing deep into Charleston Harbor in an attempt to provoke Union soldiers, and then joined a Confederate outfit known as the Palmetto Guards. Later, before dawn on April 12, 1861, the 67-year-old was the first to send a cannonball into the masonry of Fort Sumter—about a foot above the head of a Union solder named Abner Doubleday.

With the Confederacy's surrender, Ruffin foresaw a future of lost causes and victorious enemies. If he couldn't triumph, he could still be defiant and disruptive to the end. In June 1865, he carried a rifle up to his room in his son's house and wrote a final entry in his diary: "And now with my latest writing and utterance, and with what will [be] near to my latest breath, I here repeat, & would willingly proclaim, my unmitigated hatred to Yankee rule—to all political, social and business connections with Yankees, & to the perfidious, malignant, & vile Yankee race." Then he wrapped himself in the Confederate flag—literally—and pulled the trigger.

Of course, Trump also wraps himself in the flag, constantly wades in treasonous waters, fires the first shot time and again and calls it "pushing back." As it became clear that the electorate had tired of the acrimony and ineptitude, he even pondered a future without a platform from which to project his bile: "Could you imagine if I lose? I'm not going to feel so good. Maybe I'll have to leave the country, I don't know." It was either a cry for help or a warning that he may flee prosecution. Certainly, it was an indication that he wouldn't go quietly.

———

By the time I arrive at Appomattox Court House National Historic Park, the McLean House, where Grant and Lee shook hands to end a confrontation that claimed more than 600,000 lives, is half-veiled behind a milky shroud of fog. The place where peace was brokered is hard to make out. Instead, I find myself thinking of battles. Antietam and Shiloh and Gettysburg...

And Minneapolis and Portland and Kenosha...

For the past several months, headlines have been screaming warnings, almost daily, in the form of violent skirmishes that have burst up like wildfires. They seem like precursors to... something. Not just the cities ablaze, but also the conflicts featuring dueling activists who have moved far beyond angry debate. Eleven people arrested after a Times Square brawl between protesters and a pro-Trump caravan. Six people injured during a clash in San Francisco between a handful of Trump backers and a crowd demonstrating against them. A fatal shooting during clashing demonstrations in Denver. Cannonballs and rifle-muskets have been replaced by weaponized pickup trucks and pepper spray—and the occasional AR-15.

Forgive me if the Appomattox County welcome billboard—"Where Our Nation Reunited"—feels to me a bit like George W. Bush's "Mission Accomplished" sign.

Obviously, any president with a soul would attempt to deescalate the madness. Soften the rhetoric. Address the concerns on both sides. Talk down the over-testosteroned Trumpers who feel emboldened to grab their weapons, surge into cities, and take matters into their own hands. But the instigator-in-chief only embraces them. The caravan that traveled to Portland and started firing paintballs at protestors from their trucks? They're "great patriots," and it's a backlash that "cannot be unexpected" under a Democratic mayor. The 17-year-old militia-wannabe who crossed state lines and killed two people in Kenosha? It was, Trump insists, self-defense.

But Trump has crossed an even more disturbing threshold. The president of the United States is inciting violence among those who think he's their savior and thus take him at his word. And his words provoke. To quote the eminent philosopher Foghorn Leghorn, he is as subtle as a hand grenade in a barrel of oatmeal. Last June, Trump tweeted that "protesters, anarchists, agitators, looters or lowlifes" protesting in Oklahoma would face "a much different scene" than protesters in New York or Minneapolis. "Send them to Texas," replied a man from a now-deleted account. "We will show them why we say don't mess with Texas." The following month, that man—an Army sergeant—fatally shot a 28-year-old man protesting police brutality.

In the early days of the pandemic, Trump attacked Michigan Governor Gretchen Whitmer's lockdown measures by tweeting, "LIBERATE MICHIGAN!" Thirteen days later, rifle-toting protestors entered the Michigan Senate Gallery. Months later, the FBI later foiled a plot—hatched by a militia outfit ridiculously calling itself the Wolverine Watchmen—to kidnap and possibly kill the governor. Lo and behold, it turned out that a couple of them had been among the armed group that had tried to, indeed, liberate Michigan per Trump's invitation. So what did the president do? He learned nothing. His vile instincts kicked in. He doubled down on the provocation. Whitmer, he said, only days after this mother of five was targeted for trying to stymie a pandemic, "wants to be a dictator."

If Trump isn't a sociopath, then sociopathy isn't a thing.

A public servant who is supposed to protect and defend the United States—who actually (deep breath) has compared himself to Lincoln—has allowed a coalescence of defiance that actually traffics in threats to the nation's sovereignty. His acolytes channel Edmund Ruffin. Zealously xenophobic Iowa Congressman Steve King posts an internet meme: "Folks keep talking about another civil war. One side has about 8 trillion bullets, while the other side doesn't know which bathroom to use." Dumber-than-a-crawdad Louisiana Congressman Clay Higgins posts a photo of armed Black men and writes, "One way ticket fellas. Have your affairs in order. Me?... I wouldn't even spill my beer. I'd drop any 10 of you where you stand." And Trump himself, at the start of his impeachment trial, retweets this jaw-dropper: "If the Democrats are successful in removing the President from office (which they will never be), it will cause a *Civil War like fracture* in this Nation from which our Country will never heal." That's the *president* floating the possibility of rebellion against the United States.

Naturally, hashtags like *#CivilWar2* and *#CivilWarSignup* began trending on Twitter that day. But it's not a trend; it's a widespread fear. Even before 2020, a poll found that 31 percent of American voters feared that the intense partisanship and Trump's election would cause a Second Civil War within five years. Another revealed that "the average voter believes the U.S. is two-thirds of the way to the edge of a civil war." When Trump refused to commit to a peaceful transition of power should he lose re-election, *New York Times* columnist Thomas Friedman remarked, "I began my career as a journalist covering Lebanon's second civil war in its history, and I'm terrified to find myself ending my career as a journalist covering America's potential second civil war."

The scenario this time around is arguably even more upsetting. For all the romanticism about the events of 1861-65 pitting brother against brother, it was essentially a regional conflict, a war between the states. Yes, it was primarily about a principled divide regarding slavery, but thousands of non-slave-owners fought and died for the South, and at least as many fervent racists wore Union blue. However, the cold war that has heated up in 2020 is being waged along opposite spokes of an ideological wheel—America First vs. Humanity First, the Way It Has Been vs. the Way It Should Be, Consolidation of Power vs. Collective Opportunity, Perceived Realism vs. Idealism... Frankly, I believe Us vs. Them has become a referendum on the limits of self-interest—We vs. Me. A war between states inherently features boundaries, but a war between states of mind is neighbor against neighbor, fathers disowning daughters, old pals discovering that they possess diametrically opposed worldviews and measuring decades of friendship against the notion that some things are simply unforgivable. A fractured country can heal; fractured relationships might not.

The fog is beginning to lift in Appomattox, and it looks as if the rain has wiped the area clean. I walk along a gravel path, past a U.S. flag hanging limp on a flagpole, and make my way to the old brick Clover Hill Tavern, where a ranger sits in a rocking chair on the porch. He wears a straw boater hat and a face covering. For a steady parade of visitors, he happily imparts information that he must have covered countless times before.

"I was telling my grandson here," an elderly man offers through his mask as he waves toward the empty expanse of green surrounding us, "it's hard to imagine this whole place was covered with people."

The ranger nods. "Oh yeah. Lee had about thirty thousand men, and Grant had about three times as many. So we're talking a hundred-twenty-thousand soldiers here."

Later another man approaches, white-haired, his mask around his chin. "Didn't realize there was actually a battle here," he says.

"April ninth," says the ranger. "By the time it was over there were five hundred dead horses and a hundred-fifty dead men."

I peek into the gift shop, right next to the old slave quarters that are now (in what seems to be stunning tone-deafness) public restrooms. I can take Appomattox home with me: T-shirts, neckties, mugs, walking sticks, coloring books, playing cards, Confederate caps. Union caps, too. When I step back outside, a fellow in a camouflage cap is chatting up the ranger. He's probably about 30 with the short-cropped hair and long vowels of a Midwesterner. For some reason, I started to think of him as Iowa Joe, though he's probably Pete or Doug from Wisconsin or Illinois. As I'm roaming the periphery of the tavern, I hear the expert and the enthusiast banter about Civil War history—Grant's army, Sherman's march, the fact that Lee sat at the nicer marble table in McLean's house because he got there first. And then Iowa Joe posits that everybody misconstrues the impetus for the war, that all those soldiers were just a bunch of poor country boys. He shakes his head. "It's like modern politics," he says. "What you believe threatens my way of life, and if it comes down to it, I'm gonna fight for my way of life."

I'm prepared to take my leave of Appomattox, riding off like Grant and Lee, unsure of what the future holds. But I decide to drive into the historic section of the town itself, just to take a look, and I can't help but notice that the "new" Appomattox District Court House (built in 1892) is fronted by a monument "to our soldiers of the Confederacy." I park a couple of blocks away on Main Street, next to a visitor center that was once the site of an old railroad depot. Here, on April 8, 1865, Union cavalry under the command of George Armstrong Custer captured three Confederate supply trains and scattered Confederate defenders, greatly influencing Lee's decision to meet with Grant. You could say it was the beginning of the end.

But I'm unable to focus on the history because directly across the street is a historic colonial building that served as the Bank of Appomattox from 1906 to 1973. It's now an art supplies store called Jefferson Galleries, but it might be best described as a decorated manifestation of a chaotic, assertive mind. A locked door painted red shouts, in white lettering, "LAW OFFICERS PROTECT LAW ABIDERS." A sign hanging between two pillars: "Ban misogynist and anti Police speech and lyrics in public and on the airways!" Another, quoting Louis Farrakhan: "Babies having babies, black on black crime. These are plagues on the black community. Not the blue eyed devils; let them have their flag. We have more important things."

Mostly, the building offers a bizarre interspersion of opinions and oddities. Right above a gun-lover's sign—"The average response time of a 911 call is 23 minutes. The response time of a .357 is 1400 feet per second"—a cutout of Mickey Mouse stares from the second floor. Just below a ledge featuring a deceased Wicked Witch of the East is a window on which is stenciled: "1,000,000 women have been murdered and maimed in my lifetime. Without good LAW ENFORCEMENT IT WOULD HAVE BEEN FAR WORSE!" Nesting above an enormous banner shouting "HATE SPEECH IS COP KILLER MUSIC LYRICS!" are a flock of purple, plastic flamingos.

As I'm standing there, an African American man in a skullcap strides past, and our eyes meet. He shrugs. "Everyone's entitled to an opinion." Then a UPS driver rushes by in the other direction. He sees me eyeing the building and asks, "Have you talked to him?" I shake my head. He just chuckles to himself as he hurries on. I've vowed that I would be extra-careful on this journey. Few face-to-face experiences in the time of COVID, certainly not indoors if I could help it. But I can't resist. I strap on my N95 mask and step in.

"Let me know if I can help you find anything." The female voice comes from somewhere behind the rows of cards and reams of paper. I wander around a bit, just to make it look like I was browsing. Let's see... posters... packing tape... printer cartridges... a piece of the space shuttle...

Yup. It turns out that there is still a bank vault in the back of the store, its foot-thick door ajar. And in that vault, behind bars, is a NASA Robotic Shuttle Arm, serial number 0001, purchased years ago by the space buff who launched a thousand questions with the signs he placed on the front of the building. His wife got tired of seeing it in their living room, so she insisted he put it on display in the vault. He's trying to sell the robotic arm for a cool $950,000. So tucked in the back of a historic building in the heart of rural Virginia is a million-dollar space robot. It's like some surreal garage sale.

I find the friendly woman who had called to me from behind the counter. "Are you the owner?"

"Yes, I am."

"Interesting decorations outside," I begin.

She laughs quietly and nods. "It was my husband's idea."

"Is it a response to recent events?"

"Yeah. And past events. The stuff about rap music and killing women..."

She doesn't finish the thought because her husband walks in. Stefan is his name, and he is not what I expected, to say the least. Or, given the hodgepodge of attitudes and absurdities on display, maybe he's exactly what I should have expected. He's wearing a pink tie-dyed blouse and short shorts over pink tights. He's 72 years old with a deeply wrinkled face, but his straight hair is ink black, down to his shoulders. He looks like a dead-ringer for Alice Cooper. Only he has breasts. "I was born androgynous," he later explains. "Both sexes."

"We were just talking about the signs," his wife says before scurrying toward a back room. And thus begins a conversational journey unlike any I have ever had. I find Stefan to be intelligent but unnerving, affable but obdurate, prone to both empathy and prejudice (often in the same breath), broad in his historical assessments yet profoundly intimate in his personal revelations. A conversation ostensibly about law and order and protest will veer down a road with sharp turns and abrupt exits.

"I lived for years in a low-income, high-crime area," Stefan begins, sounding distinctly Yankee. "And that's where it's the law-abiding citizens and the police versus the career criminals. You cut back on the police, you're just going to make law-abiding citizens in the inner cities carry guns and everything like that. It's going to be bad. I benefited my whole life from good police."

This was in Roosevelt, New York, the Long Island suburb that has produced the likes of Dr. J, Flava Flav, Eddie Murphy, Howard Stern. One of the first integrated suburbs on Long Island, it was also one of the first to experience white flight. Lingering racism and an inequitable property tax system translated into poverty, segregation, a school system so decimated—20 percent of its teachers were quitting each year—that the state educational commissioner actually took it over a couple of decades ago.

"What cleaned up the area was... Louis Farrakhan came in. He stationed his people at each corner, and I realized that these people were actually father figures. I stopped seeing young girls get pregnant. I saw self-respect, dignity. It sure made life easier for me and other people who lived there."

"Then how did you wind up here in—"

"Some of my best friends were Black, and a couple owned a place called Tasty Take-Out, and they made so much money that they bought the plantation where their ancestors were born into slavery. And they let me know how cheap land prices were down south. So that's how I ended up here. This is an area where we all get along. There are no racial problems here. But I'll tell ya, there's a big difference between Black Muslims and Arabic Muslims. You never see Black Muslims charged with terrorism. But Arabic Muslims... and we have both sects around here, and they don't like each other."

Already my head is swimming. But I can't let his praise for a fellow who once praised Hitler go unchecked.

"Farrakhan... *really* anti-Semitic—"

"No, no, no. Here's what it is: He lambasted the Jews, but then he got educated. And he learned, it's not the Jews who were really at war with the Muslims. It's the Zionists. I lived in Massachusetts when I was younger, and I thought the Zionists were a bit on the crazy side. 'Cuz they wouldn't just say, 'See ya later.' They would say, 'Next year in Jerusalem.' But Farrakahan... He got prostate cancer, and a Jewish doctor cured him, you know. And he learned more about the Jews."

Here Stefan—obviously unaware that I descend from a long line of folks who have said "next year in Jerusalem" at every Passover seder for generations—embarks on his version of a history lesson about the Holocaust. "Hitler didn't start killing Jews right away. He just started redistributing their stuff. It's the old thing: Jesus saves, and Moses invests. So most Christians would save their money, then when inflation ran eight hundred percent, money was worthless. But investments were of value. So the Jews ended up with all the stuff because, you know... But he took it away from them and chased a lot of them to America. And then Zionists declared war on Hitler and tried to kill him. So Hitler, sort of like King Herod from the Bible, basically decided that all Jews tried to kill him. They declared war on him, and he basically decided he was going to kill all the Jews. And that was it. But think of it. All those dead Jews. The way the world felt! Ships came to America, and they sent them back! To certain death!"

This leads to stories about Israel and its various conflicts with its neighbors and how he made "so much money I didn't know what to do with it" by investing in the refinery business just before the Arab oil embargo of 1973. That might explain the space robot impulse buy. "But that meant I got out of the ghetto. Because I had two groups of people arrested for robbing me, and the first group was just getting out of jail. There's no sense being a sitting duck."

So now I think we're circling back to Appomattox. I tell him about how I'm driving across the country, how I just visited the historic McLean House, and how—just as I was musing about the jarring rhetoric on both ideological sides—I noticed the signs he posted and...

"But here's something: We have more Black customers now than we had before. Because they know. They went through the same crap I did. All these guys getting killed have records." That's what he said. I think he meant the victims of police brutality. "I'm gonna put a big sign on the back of the building that tries to unite people. It doesn't matter who you vote for president. What you really gotta do is boycott Nike. Boycott anyone who advertises on the NFL. All these things. This is all about money and power. This guy in NASCAR, Bubba Wallace, what good did it do for him to bring down the Confederate flag? It's a power trip. So I'm starting a thing to get people to say, *hey, stop paying ESPN*. You deprive them of cash, you deprive them of—"

"Why them, though?"

"Who was the first commercial place that went and endorsed all this stuff?"

"The protests, you mean?"

"No. This guy Kapatnick..."

"Kaepernick."

"Yeah, that unemployed *thing*." That's what he called a man who has been blacklisted for quietly kneeling to protest racial injustice—an unemployed thing. "See, Obama, Kapatnick, this guy Bubba... they lived in middle-class areas. They never lived in a high-crime area. They don't know what they're talking about. They never experienced it."

As I feel my blood pressure rising, I feel my eloquence plummeting. 'There are bad cops," I try. "Some very bad cops, right?"

He doesn't answer directly. "Let's take this guy who got shot in the back..."

"In Kenosha?"

"Yeah, right. Here's the thing: His girlfriend or mother or wife or whatever called the police on him. She had an order of protection. I don't know if you know how harsh family things can be, but those are volatile situations. He was violating an order of protection."

"That doesn't mean you shoot him in the back seven times..."

"Wait, wait, wait. He got into a car with three children in it. These things can get really out of control. If he would have ran off in that car and killed those kids... it happens. People get mad at someone and kill their own kids. It happens all the time."

"You're saying they should shoot him in the back just in case he drives away and hurts his kids?"

"No. Did you see the video of it? I watched it. They tried to stop him from getting in the car."

I try to change lanes. "What about George Floyd in Minneapolis? Eight minutes on his neck."

"Right. There are some cops who were probably bullied in school, and they got that badge to go out and bully people. I'd say that was excessive, yeah. You talk about bad cops? Yeah. That case, to me, that's a cop who uses the badge to abuse people."

"You'll admit, though, that it's not a lone situation. It happens a lot..."

"Where?" he says. He's incredulous, as if my statement was even the least bit hyperbolic.

"Everywhere."

"Well, what's your experience with cops?"

"It doesn't matter what *my* experience has been. I'm white. When I get stopped for speeding, I don't have to worry about getting shot."

This leads Stefan to a story from decades earlier where he tried to stop some drunk white guys from accusing a Black guy of stealing a car, and the cops came, and pointed guns at all of them. "So I'm saying I got pulled over a lot..."

"But you don't get shot."

"I don't resist arrest! They're supposed to take control of the situation. That's what they're taught in the academy."

If he sees no daylight between taking control and taking a life, we're at an impasse. "So... the people who are traveling to where the protests are with an AR-15... how do you feel about that?"

"Well, if it's your own backyard... like, for instance, we had a demonstration here, and the cops came in and told my wife the protests are coming, there's plenty of police protection, so I figured me with a gun here is detrimental to the cops because there are so many of them here. But if they didn't protect the area, I would have been in there with a gun, yeah."

"What if you heard there was a protest in, let's say, Richmond. Would you go there with a gun?"

"No. No."

"So why the hell did that kid do that in Kenosha? He was seventeen..."

"He lived there!"

"No. He was from Illinois. He got driven to the area. By his mom."

Stefan shrugs. "Yeah. I don't think he'll get convicted at all. Think of it. Two guys came at him. You gotta be nuts to go after a young person with a gun. They're the worst kind. I'm not in favor of anyone under twenty-one buying a gun. But I can understand what was going on there. If it happened right here and there was no police protection... I have plenty of guns."

These days, that's a frighteningly common refrain. Across the country, gun sales are booming. Ammunition is sold out. During the first eight months of this year, there were nearly as many background checks conducted nationally—some 15 million—as there had been in any full year in history. One restaurant owner in rural California challenged government officials to just try and enforce a pandemic shutdown order. "I've made it very clear that if they come to shut us down, I'm going to call 100,000 people that'll be there with guns, and what happens happens, you know?" he said. "Right now, we're being peaceful. But it's not going to be peaceful much longer." Indeed, much of the Left's fear regarding violence in the wake of the presidential election revolves around the notion that "they have all the guns." But there has been an influx of first-time gun buyers—nearly double that in past years—because progressives are stocking up on guns, too. Anxiety knows no ideology.

The question hanging over the conflict like a storm cloud is not only whether or not the skirmishes proliferating throughout the country are symptoms or precursors, but also how far the chasm is between threats and actions. I figure Stefan is more of the former. But I figure wrong. There's a pause in the conversation. And then, this...

"I've actually shot nine people. So... you're talking to the Long Island Shooter. That's me."

I'm certain I didn't hear him correctly. "Did you say... Wait, what?"

"I shot 'em. They were attacking me. They were all white and wealthy."

I don't even know how to respond, or whether to even pull on this thread. "You mean you shot at nine people, right? You didn't actually *shoot* nine people."

"No. I shot 'em. They got double-0 buckshot in their calves."

"I don't understand. Nine? All at one time?"

"No." That would be preposterous. "Three, three, and three. See, that's why we live here. It was the 1980s, and cocaine was a big epidemic in the community. And these guys would get high on cocaine and alcohol, and even when cops would drive by they would throw rocks and break the cops' windows. And just smirk."

"So... how did... what did these nine people have against you in particular?"

"Um, they would go crazy in the community, just destroying houses. It first started with this one guy who owned an Italian restaurant. They would go and break the windows in his house. He would catch them and get them arrested. And one day, they beat him up so bad with baseball bats that he ended up in a hospital for a few months. And while he was there, they burned his house to the ground. But I thought, well, maybe this is an Italian thing... Then they went into the house of the people across the street and did so much damage they knocked down the interior supporting walls so the roof started caving in. They were a homosexual couple who lived in New York City and only came out for the weekends. So I thought maybe they didn't like homosexuals. Then they started with me. That was a mistake. I have a gun. I used a gun effectively on Long Island for years. Very effectively. And so, that was it. And every one of these guys was white."

Good thing my mask was keeping my jaw in place. "And it happened three different times?"

"Yep. The last time, two of the guys I shot, their father was a big mob attorney. And then a few months later, my neighbor a few blocks over was killed in a hit. The cops came to me and said, 'This guy didn't have an enemy in the world. But his biggest mistake was he had a van just like yours.' I tried to keep them at a distance. I put up heavy fencing, barbed wire, bulletproof windows. Finally, this detective said, 'We know he did it. We know he killed the wrong guy. But it's time for you got get out of Dodge.'"

It's time for me to do the same. Stefan is a reminder that the broad coalitions marching toward conflict in America are made up of individuals fighting their own demons, their own personal traumas and histories that inform their ideologies. In his case, I don't know where the truth ends and exaggeration begins. Is he predictably dogmatic or uncategorizable? Does he espouse well-meaning paternalism or racism? Does he seem to rationalize anti-Semitism while believing he's above it? Does he own an inflated sense of injustice, or is he somewhat justified in his claims to persecution?

Gosh, again, all of that reminds me of someone...

With a wide smile, he thanks me for the visit and bids me farewell. As I open the door and squint into the late afternoon sun, I hear him behind me. "I hope you don't drive into any riots! Peace to you!"

LOST CAUSE

HAZARD, KENTUCKY

Today, I curve along county highways into the heart of Appalachia. Past Abingdon and Hansonville and St. Paul, where the trees and cliffsides that loom over the highway are smothered in kudzu, like frozen green waterfalls. Past the lonely, rural Midway Church, which begs the question: Midway between what? Past the Trinity Life Center near the hamlet of Bald Knob, where the marquee sadly implores, "Pray for our students and teachers." Past the University of Virginia's College at Wise—a location as much as an aspiration. Past a morning radio show billboard near the town of Pound: "Jesus and Coffee." Past the Payne Gap church marquee: "The world is changed by your example, not your opinion."

I rise over a pass and into Kentucky, then down, down, down as rain suddenly starts falling in sheets. So I rest at a park in Whitesburg. "Population 1534 friendly people and 2 grouches," says the welcome billboard. Whitesburg was named for a local politician named White. I had to check, just to make sure, which bothers me. There's a sign in town, the first Democratic banner I've noticed along my entire journey. "Vote Amy McGrath for U.S. Senate." She's an earnest, likeable former fighter pilot campaigning against Mitch McConnell, a 78-year-old sycophant with the personality of a bran muffin. Current polls show her losing.

Onward. Over gorgeous Carr Creek Lake. Past a pair of hamlets that sound like *Little Rascals* characters to me—Vicco and Sassafrass. And three more consecutive hiccups that suggest some sort of dystopian *Snow White*—Scuddy, Happy, and Jeff. And finally into Hazard, Kentucky.

Yes, that Hazard, the one made famous by Daisy and Uncle Jesse and Bo and Luke Duke. Sure, *The Dukes of Hazzard* was set in Georgia—in a fictional Hazzard with two Z's. Kentucky's Hazard was named for an early 19th-century naval commander, but the city embraced the association with a hit show that inexplicably attracted some 45 million weekly viewers at its peak. There used to be a Dukes of Hazzard Steakhouse in town. And a pool hall called Boss Hogg's Place. And one Perry County judge used to ride around town in a shiny white Cadillac—Hogg-like, decked out in a white hat and suit and chomping on a huge cigar. Well, until he was indicted on 41 charges, including mail fraud and arson. "Hazzard County was a fictional thing," said Ben Jones, who played the mechanic Cooter on the show and who was made an honorary citizen by the city. "But we always related to Hazard, Kentucky, because that's the real deal."

The TV stars embraced Hazard, too. In fact, when several of the supporting actors served as grand marshals for the city's Black Gold Festival in 1981, some 70,000 fans greeted them in a city of roughly 5,000 residents. "Biggest thing to ever hit Hazard," said one lifelong resident. John Schneider, who played Bo, later visited. "The best moonshine I ever had came out of the impound closet in Hazard, Kentucky," he recalled. In 1982, after a mine explosion killed eight local miners, Tom Wopat (Luke) showed up to present a $25,000 check from Warner Brothers for the victims' families.

My surname means "duke" in German. I named my first child Luke. We almost named him Bo. My other son is named Jesse. Either those are silly coincidences, or *The Dukes of Hazzard* is embedded in my subconscious. However, as innocent and mindless as the show may have been, it simply wouldn't fly today because what everyone remembers most is the now-cringeworthy car they drove—a 1969 Dodge Charger, bright orange, 01 on the side, greased hood, no windows. They called it the "General Lee," and there was a big Confederate flag painted on the roof.

As bad taste goes, it's not nearly as offensive as *Heil Honey, I'm Home*, a 1990 British sitcom that lasted all of one episode before folks decided that a show about a 1950s-style Hitler family with Jewish neighbors was... maybe not the best idea. But through a 21st-century lens, an action-comedy about a couple of bootleggers outrunning the law in a car adorned with what is widely interpreted as a symbol of oppression and slavery... maybe not the best idea either. The show's creator, a guy named Gy Waldron, who is now pushing 90, has insisted that when he was growing up in Kentucky "no one even connected the Confederate flag with slavery. It was simply a part of our Southern culture." And when the Dukes were a top-rated tandem, folks didn't seem to mind the Stars and Bars so much. Hazard's citizens waved the flag enthusiastically as the actors who played Daisy and Sheriff Roscoe P. Coltrane and deputies Cletus and Enos inched past them along the parade route.

But the landscape has changed—and I think it's mostly because folks finally realize that the meaning of the Confederate flag *hasn't*.

In 2015, a psychopath posed with that and other symbols of white supremacy before gunning down nine Black churchgoers in Charleston. In the ensuing days, then-Governor Nikki Haley removed the flag from the South Carolina statehouse grounds. But four years later, amid Trump trumpeting the "misrepresentation" of the symbol and after Haley decided to set up camp on the Dark Side, she felt the need to defend the Blood-Stained Banner. She claimed that the killer "hijacked" the flag from people who saw it as symbolizing "service, and sacrifice and heritage." If she ever runs for president, let that steaming pile of revisionism follow her along.

Just days after the murderous spree, journalist Ta-Nehisi Coates wrote a compelling and comprehensive piece for *The Atlantic* in which he examined the real-time attitudes of the South before and during the Civil War, the driving force behind the Confederacy, and thus the meaning of its most salient symbol. His conclusion: "The Confederate flag should not come down because it is offensive to African Americans. The Confederate flag should come down because it is embarrassing to all Americans." His evidence: the very words of the Confederates themselves.

He cited a declaration, two years before Lincoln's election, from a U.S. senator from Mississippi, who talked of annexing Cuba and parts of Mexico: "I want these countries for the spread of slavery. I would spread the blessings of slavery, like the religion of our Divine Master, to the uttermost ends of the earth." Coates also uncovered a sorry piece of spittle from Georgia's governor, just before the state seceded: "Among us the poor white laborer is respected as an equal. His family is treated with kindness, consideration and respect. He does not belong to the menial class. The negro is in no sense of the term his equal. He feels and knows this. He belongs to the only true aristocracy, the race of white men."

As the war progressed, however, perpetuation of human bondage proved to be a tough sell when trying to muster support from abroad, so Confederate diplomats started to reframe the battle cry: States' rights, not slavery. It wasn't just a reimagination of Confederate inspirations; it was a rebranding. But Coates pierced that myth by simply quoting excerpts from the actual Declaration of Causes of Secession—literally, the here's-why-we're-fighting manifestos—in no uncertain terms.

South Carolina: "A geographical line has been drawn across the Union, and all the States north of that line have united in the election of a man to the high office of President of the United States, whose opinions and purposes are hostile to slavery."

Louisiana: "The people of the slave holding States are bound together by the same necessity and determination to preserve African slavery."

Mississippi: "Our position is thoroughly identified with the institution of slavery—the greatest material interest of the world. Its labor supplies the product which constitutes by far the largest and most important portions of commerce of the earth. These products are peculiar to the climate verging on the tropical regions, and by an imperious law of nature, none but the Black race can bear exposure to the tropical sun... a blow at slavery is a blow at commerce and civilization... There was no choice left us but submission to the mandates of abolition, or a dissolution of the Union."

Texas: "...the servitude of the African race, as existing in these States, is mutually beneficial to both bond and free, and is abundantly authorized and justified by the experience of mankind, and the revealed will of the Almighty Creator, as recognized by all Christian nations; while the destruction of the existing relations between the two races, as advocated by our sectional enemies, would bring inevitable calamities upon both and desolation upon the fifteen slave-holding states....

And this lovely gem of enlightenment from Alabama: "...the election of Mr. Lincoln cannot be regarded otherwise than a solemn declaration, on the part of a great majority of the Northern people, of hostility to the South, her property and her institutions—nothing less than an open declaration of war—for the triumph of this new theory of Government destroys the property of the South, lays waste her fields, and inaugurates all the horrors of a San Domingo servile insurrection, consigning her citizens to assassinations, and her wives and daughters to pollution and violation, to gratify the lust of half-civilized Africans."

In the decades that followed, even well into the 20th century, the *Confederate Veteran*—the official publication of the United Confederate Veterans—lamented the Lost Cause. But not on behalf of the slave owners; rather, regarding the slaves. In 1906: "The kindliest relation that ever existed between the two races in this country, or that ever will, was the ante-bellum relation of master and slave." In 1911: "The thoughtful and considerate negro of to-day realizes his indebtedness to the institution of African slavery for advantages which he would not have received had he remained in his semi-barbarism waiting in his native jungles for the delayed missionary." In 1917: "Great and trying times always produce great leaders, and one was at hand—Nathan Bedford Forrest. His plan, the only course left open. The organization of a secret government... known in history as the Ku Klux Klan."

Slavery was lost, but racial segregation and white dominion became the new southern mission shammed as a states' rights issue. Coates discovered a Florida senator who declared, in 1931, " The South fought to preserve race integrity. Did we lose that? We fought to maintain free white dominion. Did we lose that?... I submit that what is called 'The Lost Cause' was not so much 'lost' as is sometimes supposed." The senator added, "The glorious blood-red Confederate Battle Flag that streamed ahead of the Confederate soldiers in more than 2000 battles is not a conquered banner."

Time marched on, and eventually slavery and subjugation were folded into a much more benign-sounding devotion. Heritage was the new word. "Heritage Not Hate." And that battle flag? As one former politician put it in a 2015 op-ed for *The New York Times*, "To those 70 million of us whose ancestors fought for the South, it is a symbol of family members who fought for what they thought was right in their time, and whose valor became legendary in military history."

Fought for what they thought was right? I recently discovered an ancestral fact that had been unknown to my extended family: My great-great-uncle spent some time in the First U.S. Cavalry. Records show that he was an "Indian fighter." I think it's exotic, particularly in a branch of my family that produced mostly Midwestern dry cleaners. I think it's fascinating how he went from Hungary to Idaho... and eventually to San Francisco, just before the big 1906 quake. I think his history is worth knowing. But an Indian fighter? I'm not proud of it, and I certainly wouldn't raise a flag to celebrate it.

That op-ed writer, by the way, was Ben Jones. Cooter, it turns out, was a two-term Democratic congressman from Georgia and the "chief of heritage operations" for the Sons of Confederate Veterans. Yup. "It is obvious that some racists have appropriated and desecrated the Confederate battle flag for their pathetic causes," he wrote, "but those hateful folks also commonly display the Christian cross and the American flag. Do those symbols also inspire racism?"

Well, Cooter... that's a bit like saying, "Hey, the Nazis commonly wore brown shirts. Lots of people wear brown shirts. Are those deemed anti-Semitic? No? So what's wrong with a swastika?"

This past summer, Jones sat for an interview with Fox News. Of course, by then TV Land had announced that it was pulling reruns of his old show because of the flag controversy. Warner Brothers had stopped selling products featuring the Stars and Bars, including *Dukes of Hazzard* merchandise. The Mississippi legislature had voted to remove the Confederate battle emblem from the state flag after 126 years. And even NASCAR—for crying out loud, NASCAR—had banned the flag from its races and properties. Naturally, Trump criticized the move.

In his interview, Jones—who once worked a railroad job in Hazard, some 60 years ago—contended that the whole anti-Stars-and-Bars movement was a case of judging the past by the present, that it constituted cultural cleansing, that a "rebellious spirit" was the primary connotation of the Confederate flag. "I've lived in the South all my life and I ain't seen them since the 1960s, really," Jones said in an interview. Those flags, he added, "ain't here anymore."

Uh-huh. Okay. I've decided to test that claim with a visit to this hard-to-reach outpost nestled in a wooded valley. But is it fair to Hazard, Kentucky?

A reputation is hard to shake, warranted or not. Hazard has its past. In 1934, the town was the scene of the state's last public lynching. After a Black man beat a white miner to death in a bar fight, he was dragged from jail and hanged from a sassafras tree. Kentucky's 5th congressional district, including Hazard, has the highest percentage of white Americans in the nation. Its representative, Republican Hal Rogers, has been given a 28 percent rating from the NAACP on his civil rights voting record and a zero percent rating from the Human Rights campaign. Both sides of the aisle find him to be an embarrassment. *Rolling Stone* named him one of America's "Ten Worst Congressmen." Citizens for Responsibility and Ethics in Washington named him to its list of the "Most Corrupt Members of Congress." The *National Review* called him "a national disgrace." He has been elected and re-elected 20 times in a row, ever since 1980.

And yet... when Hazard High School elected its first Black homecoming queen, an AP headline gushed, "Race Relations in Mountain Town Seen as Model." If you work in the coal mines, you're equal, the residents said. Bonded by common struggles. The story marveled at how the newly-crowned queen could walk down the street while holding the hand of her white boyfriend, and nobody would bat an eye. Of course, this was in 1995, not 1955. Low bars allow high praise.

However, only a couple of months ago, as I write this, the *Hazard Herald* offered this judgment-free report about a truly touching event: "On June 6, a peaceful protest held in Hazard drew hundreds of people together to march in support of the Black Lives Matter movement, to honor all the lives that have been lost due to racism and to protest police brutality." People of color make up less than 10 percent of the coalfield city's population. The organizers didn't think 50 people would show. They got 500, mostly white, of all ages and from throughout the county, marching in solidarity, holding signs. DEFEND BLACK LIVES. UNITED WE STAND. RESPECT EXISTENCE OR EXPECT RESISTANCE. Featured speakers included the mayor, members of the sheriff department, and the Reverend Steven Jones, who remarked that he had lived his entire life as a Black man in Hazard and had never seen anything like that collective show of support. Toward the end of the march, everyone knelt for eight minutes and 46 seconds—the amount of time George Floyd was tortured by Derek Chauvin before he died in Minneapolis. All involved remarked that it felt like a *very* long time.

So I find myself looking forward to Hazard. I coast into town, and moments later I stop near what looks to be an abandoned white building festooned in big red letters: HAZARD VENDORS MALL. Time and the elements have worn away the middle two letters of HAZARD. So it just reads... HARD, which aptly describes life in this old mining town. In fact, Kentucky's 5th is the second most impoverished district in America. But I knew I'd find that.

No, I've decided I'm here for one reason only. I need a dose of hopefulness, and I fully expect to conclude that it's generally unfair—metaphorically speaking—to paint a town with the same colors used to adorn the Duke brothers' General Lee. So I've assigned myself a silly mission, but one designed to lift my spirits: I'm going to see if I can spot a Confederate flag. Afflicted with a rare case of optimism, I don't think I'll find a single one.

It takes me all of thirty seconds.

Glancing to my right, I discover that I'm parked in front of a low slung building of painted red bricks—the new Hazard Vendors location. "Pickers Paradise," says one sign. "We buy junk," says another. Several banners hang in the store's front windows: an American flag; a "Don't Tread on Me" flag showing a coiled rattlesnake on a yellow field—the Gadsen flag coopted by the American Tea Party; a "Re-elect Donald Trump Keep America Great" flag; a depiction of Trump standing atop a marauding tank with fireworks exploding in the background; and finally, a hybrid flag—half Old Glory, half Stars and Bars. There are a handful of rusted shovels on display, too, presumably for all the garbage they're peddling.

As the bile rises in my throat, with a mask across my face, I walk inside and find shelves brimming with cat food and motor oil and tile cleaner and adult diapers, rows of condiments and cake mixes and Slim Jims and barbecued-flavored potato chips, collections of cheap jewelry and sweatsuits and tool sets and Hot Wheels cars. But about eight steps in—literally almost immediately—I notice a table topped with a Stars and Bars flag, a Stars and Bars blanket, Stars and Bars window decals, Stars and Bars napkins emblazoned with REDNECK, and a license plate frame with the Stars and Bars overlaid with an outline of an assault rifle and a threat: COME AND TAKE IT. They're all sitting next to several packages of "You Can Be Anything" Barbie dolls. Apparently, you can be a racist troll.

I get out of there as soon as possible. Not the vendors mall. I mean Hazard.

I know it's not fair. As I drive through town, I'm aware of many fine things about the place. There's a pleasant fountain next to City Hall. Several colorful murals liven up the drear here and there, a product of the Appalachian Arts Alliance. There's a building constructed to look like a goose—the Mother Goose Inn. Charming. And I don't glimpse one other Stars and Bars—not in a yard, not in a window, not on a bumper sticker. Instead, dozens of Stars and Stripes line the business district alongside banners: QUEEN CITY OF THE MOUNTAINS.

But it's nearly 90 degrees and oppressively humid. The sky is growing late. Covfefe is sounding angry. And I'm demoralized. So I continue west, climbing aboard a toll road that takes me toward the setting sun. It's called the Hal Rogers Parkway.

GOD HELP US

SCIENCE HILL, KENTUCKY

A few years back, a talented artist pal of mine was commissioned to paint a 10-by-3 foot depiction of all of the presidents lined up together as if waiting for a parade to pass by. Lincoln standing tall. Teddy Roosevelt and Taft laughing it up. Richard Nixon brooding. This was before the 2016 election. You can tell because Obama is reaching out a hand to an unseen newcomer. And he's smiling. So you know he's not about to welcome to the club a guy who incorporates all the very worst traits of various presidents who preceded him—Nixon's paranoia, Warren Harding's corruption, Woodrow Wilson's racism, LBJ's narcissism, John Adams's vanity, Bill Clinton's infidelity, George W. Bush's incuriosity, James Buchanan's indifference, Andrew Johnson's incompetence, and Andrew Jackson's cruelty. But anyway... the painting is fantastic. To accompany each presidential image, he asked me to write a few hundred words on each POTUS, and we produced a coffee table book called—how's this for clever?—*The Presidents*.

Recently, we embarked on a follow-up project for the Wyoming Museum of Science and Industry. I was asked to help compile a diverse list of 60 names—geniuses from all of human history—who make the cut for a collection called *The Thinkers*. Consider the challenge. Who rank among the most influential innovators and scientists? Which developments and discoveries most merit inclusion? Aside from the first-ballot Hall of Famers—Galileo, da Vinci, Einstein, Curie, Edison, the Wright brothers—who are the game-changers? It's an impossible task, of course, but we did our best to be clever and comprehensive. So the painting shows George Washington Carver seated between Ben Franklin and Stephen Hawking, Jane Goodall looking over Charles Darwin's shoulder, Johannes Gutenberg standing alongside Cherokee alphabet inventor Sequoyah, and Steve Jobs on a balcony... dropping an apple toward Isaac Newton.

But as we compiled the collection, I realized that this was an opportunity to make a statement. Presidents are presidents, whether we like it or not, but this was a subjective list. We could choose not only who we celebrated, but why. That's why I lobbied to leave out the likes of rabid anti-Semite Henry Ford, racist "Father of DNA" James Watson, and slavery enabler Eli Whitney. Instead, we opted for activists and environmentalists like Temple Grandin, Rachel Carson, and Nobel Peace Prize winner Wangari Maathai.

And that's why we included Dr. Anthony Fauci.

Sure, one could argue that his work during the AIDS crisis alone merits consideration. But there is a more basic reason for his appearance in the painting. We're simply saying: Respect the scientific method. Believe the experts. Science saves lives. It seems obvious, but COVID-19 has revealed that this notion is threatened by a nation's prideful ignorance. The U.S. has become a coronavirus cautionary tale to the rest of the world. A failure. Not because of our size, but because of our hubris.

It starts at the top, of course. With 20/20 hindsight, one might wonder if there was some sort of blueprint for bungling a health crisis—as if, like Max Bialystock in *The Producers*, seeking the worst play ever written, Trump asked his advisors to game out the poorest possible response to a pandemic. Horrified at the task but certain that it would never see the light of day, the strategists compiled a 20-Point Plan that would assure more than a quarter of a million dead Americans by the end of the year.

How To Bungle A National Health Crisis

1. **Undermine preparedness.** Eliminate the White House National Security Council's Directorate for Global Health Security and Biodefense. Fire the head of pandemic response and disband his team. Cut a program that tracks emerging pathogens around the globe.

2. **Ignore warnings.** Shrug off alarming briefings from administration intelligence and health expert during the first two critical months. Dismiss initial signs of the pandemic as transient.

3. **Don't trust the general public.** Minimize the crisis to avoid panic—not as a safety issue, but solely to protect an economy that you believe is your only chance for re-election. Compare the coronavirus to the common flu, when you know it's far worse. Tell people in the path of a viral hurricane that it's just going to be a stiff breeze for a while.

4. **Fail math.** Reveal a total lack of understanding of the exponential nature of a pandemic. Say something like, "We only have fifteen cases here, and pretty soon we're going to get that down to zero."

5. **Ignore reality.** Describe the coronavirus as "very much under control" when it's just starting. As the number of infections plateau and then rise again, declare victory and move on. Employ magical thinking. Articulate your secret desires, and frame them as expert predictions: It should weaken by April. It doesn't like hot weather. It will soon disappear "like a miracle."

6. **Abdicate leadership.** Instead of crafting a unified federal response and a national infrastructure for testing and tracing, leave it up to state, local, and private actors to solve the country's greatest health crisis. Pit them against each other. Then bash those seeking more federal help.

7. **Politicize a pandemic.** Call criticism of your slow response another Democratic hoax. When the pandemic hits urban areas and blue states hard, criticize Democratic mayors and governors. Pretend to take the situation seriously only when it starts to hit rural and red places.

8. **Avoid any hint of empathy.** With many unemployed Americans relying on Obamacare after losing job-based insurance, try to scrap the Affordable Care Act. When the death totals become jaw-dropping, shrug and say, "It is what it is." And when a reporter asks you what you would say to Americans who are scared, answer, "I'd say you're a terrible reporter."

9. **Create a circus.** In your first big press performance upon deeming it a national emergency, surround yourself with a hastily-assembled gaggle of CEOs. Make sure to shake everyone's hand. Hold daily press briefings in which medical advice is trumped by the ramblings of a pathological narcissist. Meander into unintelligible verbal cul-de-sacs.

10. **Prioritize your political future over public safety.** Trot out optimistic but misleading claims and statistics. Hint that a vaccine is just around the corner, when only the election is. Promote unproven and even dangerous approaches. Like injecting disinfectant. Violate state mandates by scheduling super-spreader campaign rallies where face masks and social distancing are as common as BLM banners.

11. **Lie, constantly.** Amid a deadly global plague, when honesty and clarity of facts are paramount, offer hearsay, repeat rumors, conflate information. "Anybody that needs a test, gets a test." Google engineers are building a testing website. Obama left a "bad" and "obsolete" test... for a virus that didn't exist when he was in office. The pandemic is "fading away." Some 99% of COVID-19 cases are "totally harmless." Children are "virtually immune." We have the "lowest fatality rate in the world."

12. **Embolden toxic masculinity.** When the CDC recommends masks for public use, describe it as a personal choice, refuse to wear one in public, and mock your opponent for doing so. Don't ask your supporters to sacrifice even in the form of minor lifestyle changes. Pander to what you know best—dismissing selflessness as weakness.

13. **Make it all about you.** Reframe fear and criticism of your performance as yet another attempt to bring you down. Suggest that people are wearing masks to spite you. Decry tougher vaccine standards as a political move. Spin every question about what can be done better into a spewing of what you've done right. When the questions start getting too challenging, simply cancel your daily briefings.

14. **Put out mixed messages.** Undercut your administration's enforcement protocols. Tell people to social distance, then don't model it. Call it a national emergency, then say it's overblown. Give lip service to stay at home orders, then call for all churches to be filled on Easter Sunday.

15. **Circumvent logic.** When the numbers start rising ominously, blame it on too much testing, as if breast cancer is widespread because we offer too many mammograms. "So I said to my people, 'Slow the testing down, please.'"

16. **Rush to reopen.** Urge Republican-led states to resume widespread economic activity even though they fail to meet federal guidelines. And when Democratic governors follow CDC guidelines regarding shutdowns, tweet "LIBERATE" to light a fire under your ill-informed army.

17. **Move the goalposts.** Disingenuously reset expectations when the numbers become too shocking too shrug off. Make a sudden pivot into saying that keeping the death toll under 200,000 will constitute a "good job." And when even that tragic bar is exceeded...

18. **Slough off accountability.** Don't let the buck stop with you: "I don't take responsibility at all." But blame everyone else: your predecessor, your critics, the press... and, of

course, Fauci. Slowly vilify the top infectious disease scientist in the US government in the midst of a pandemic to such an extent he needs a security detail because the president's supporters, egged on by the man himself, see him as some sort of enemy obstacle.

19. **Remember to enable racism.** Find a way, somehow, to inject a dollop of bigotry and xenophobia into the narrative. Turn fears into scapegoating. Blame Mexican immigrants for infecting the American Southwest. Call it the Chinese Virus. Or better yet, the Kung Flu. While one thousand people a day are still dying, try to change the subject with dog-whistle rhetoric that stokes a race war. Try to make Americans fear each other more than a plague.

And finally:

20. **Sow doubts about science.** Impugn the credibility of top scientific institutions in the midst of a pandemic. Undermine the CDC. Attack the FDA. Defund the WHO. Disagree with your own experts. Attack the press whenever they try to separate scientific facts from seat-of-your-pants fiction. Then choose your own truth. Call testing "a double-edged sword." Muse that masks can be harmful. Muzzle any scientific voices at odds with your self-aggrandizing version of reality.

This one has been a long time coming. For years, America has been spawning an army of dunderheads—soldiers of science-denial who march into the fray with great fanfare and stand at rigid inattention. Captain Anti-Evolutionist. Private Flat Earther. Major Anti-Vaxxer. But it all has become more existentially dangerous now that General Denial has shrugged off action against climate change and dismissed expertise about COVID-19. Now this ignoramus army has found a commander-in-chief. And his most trusted foot soldiers are outspoken evangelicals, who claim to follow the word of God but have all but deified a truly godless human.

Science and religion have always had a tenuous relationship, as believers in each hold it up as the highest authority, intractably so. There was a time, of course, when the world found it difficult to distinguish between the two—when superstition and rumor were considered viable medical options. A pandemic raged, and everything resembling normality was disrupted. Once-mundane activities became fraught with tragic possibilities. Widespread fear fed mistreatment of the poor and disenfranchised. People fled from the disease or isolated themselves or died alone or among strangers. Business ground to a halt. And defiant preachers assembled their faithful, promising false hope through divine intervention, preying on desperation, calling it praying.

That was during the Black Death—in the so-called Dark Ages. But here and now, amid a once-a-century plague, there seems to have been a resurgence in the cold war between fact and faith. In the 21st century, when we can sequence genomes and transplant hearts and retrieve images of Saturn's moons, there are still headlines like this:

CHRISTIAN LEADERS CALL ON FELLOW BELIEVERS TO TAKE SCIENCE SERIOUSLY DURING THE PANDEMIC

As Christian legal defenders have pushed for churches to reopen ahead of public health parameters, as high-profile pastors and mega-churches have openly flouted restrictions, it can seem like the Right to Life folks are advocating a Right to Die. There is no question that communal congregation can be healing, in a manner of speaking, during times of disorder and despair. But much of the rhetoric in defense of in-person worship appears to prioritize the practice of religion over its message. Pastor Rodney Howard-Browne, who leads Revival Ministries International, said, "The only time the church will close is when the Rapture is taking place." He then added this sushi roll of raw denial wrapped in toxic masculinity: "This Bible school is open because we're raising up revivalists, not pansies."

And, of course, there are those on the extremes who have found solace in religious bigotry. Believers have always turned to faith in an attempt to answer the "Why?" of tragedy. If God wouldn't cause it, if science and randomness don't satisfy, it must be the fault of the "others." In the 1300s, the Jews—history's scapegoat—were largely blamed for the plague. Seven centuries later, in a blog post titled "Is God Judging America Today?", a pastor who leads a weekly Bible study group for members of Trump's Cabinet appeared to cast the pandemic as God's wrath brought on by atheists, environmentalists, and those who have "a proclivity toward lesbianism and homosexuality."

He's an idiot. But maybe he's a symptom, too—of another condition in which attitudes are driven more by ideology than theology. Amid anti-government fervor that casts any limitations on worship services as an abridgment of fundamental religious freedoms, intolerance leads to intransigence, and distrust breeds distrust. It's likely that the polarization about science is mostly politicization, another salvo in the culture wars.

All of this weighs heavily on me as I roll into a Kentucky hamlet that is home to only 696 people. But they have options—six churches in the span of about one square mile, all in a little place known as Science Hill. The juxtaposition is too inviting to pass up.

The town's little claim to fame is that it was referenced in the 2014 movie *Edge of Tomorrow* as the hometown of Master Sergeant Farell (played by Bill Paxton). When Farell is asked how Science Hill got its name, he replies, "Never asked. Don't care." But actually, it was named a century and a half ago by a geologist who had visited to gather and analyze rocks. He seems to have had the imagination of limestone.

I pull to a stop beneath the big SCIENCE HILL water tower, which looms over Science Hill City Hall and the Science Hill fire department and the Science Hill public library and post office. It's all neatly packed into a two-block bundle. I wander a bit—past an abandoned store front that still whispers DICK'S USED CARS, which is along Dick Street, which takes me to Dick's General Store. It turns out that the longtime mayor was a fellow named Bill Dick. Everything is closed and quiet, the only sound coming from the occasional freight train passing by a few dozen feet away.

I cross the street, and I'm standing in front of an impressive red-brick United Methodist Church. Along with RV repair bills and gas receipts, I've been collecting church marquee witticisms during my excursion. I'm a sucker for Dad jokes about the Holy Father. "Life without God is like an unsharpened pencil. No point."... "Ready or not, here I come. – Jesus."... "Skip rope, not church. C U Sunday."... And a particular favorite, on a 95-degree day: "Actually it's not hot as hell." The marquee in front of the Methodist Church is more crafty than quippy: "We look back and thank God. We look forward and trust God!"

But there doesn't seem to be anybody home. At the church, I mean. Apparently, Sunday school will be held at 9:45, worship at 10:40. But this is a drizzly Thursday afternoon. A sign on the front door explains, "We are practicing social distancing. Get your temperature. Please keep your distance. Wear a mask. Do not shake hands..." and then, in thick capital letters: "THE MAIN THING IS TO WORSHIP THE LORD!" I peek inside and a table by the front door holds a box of tissues, a jug of hand sanitizer, and a Bible. In other words, "Trust God!" But just in case...

As I ramble around town, from church to church, I find them empty of activity. At the large Nazarene Church, where signs in the window offer much the same message: 1) Masks are optional, 2) Sanitize your hands, 3) Stay home if you have a fever, 4) Learn about Jesus, see your teachers and friends, and have fun! But... empty, just like the Church of Christ on the other side of the railroad tracks (which offers "social distancing protocols" along with Lord's Supper prepackaged materials on a table in the foyer) and the Christian Church half a mile up Highway 27. Even at the little white house along Stanford Street where, next to signs offering a wash-and-wax for $50 and lawnmower blade sharpening for $5, there's a display—a cradle for Baby Jesus, a cross, and a question: "ARE YOU SAVED?"

Saved? I can't locate a soul.

Two blocks away from the Methodist Church is another red-brick house of worship, Northside Baptist Church. I stroll around the building's perimeter, beneath an American flag flying between two stained glass windows, past yet another marquee—"I sought the Lord and He heard me and delivered me from my fears!" I fear I'm about to be 0-for-6 until I reach a back lot and...

"Can I help you with something?"

It startles me, but it doesn't sound accusatory. Rather, sincere. The voice belongs to Tommy Claunch, a fellow in his sixties, who turns out to be thoroughly likeable with a giggle that makes you want to join in. Only six months earlier, he might have invited me inside, but half-a-year feels like an eternity these days. We stand at the back door, in a parking lot, six feet apart, and briefly discuss faith and fate. Maybe it's the proper setting.

Tommy is retired from General Electric. He's originally from down the road in Somerset, but "married a girl from up in here." He's been a member of the church for just over 30 years. "Of course, nobody's hardly ever down here these days here except for funerals. This is just the second one we've had since all this started up," he drawls. A burial. Which leads me to ask him how the church is handling COVID. "Right now, what we're having is Sunday morning services. In person. For the most part, everybody wears masks. We have every other pew taped off. Course, there's probably ten or eleven in our immediate family that go here, and we can all sit together if we choose to."

"And by immediate you mean..."

"Well, nieces and nephews and stuff like that. After services, we've got two guys that spray everything down in the sanctuary. And then after we get done tonight, we'll spray all the tables down. We use food-safe disinfectant."

I'm reminded of another church marquee that I'd noticed a few days earlier—at another First Baptist Church, actually: "Jesus cleans the heart. We disinfect the pews." These churches in Science Hill seem to be doing their best, at least, to walk the line between safety and spirituality. But I have to ask: "You don't fear going to church in person?"

He shakes his head. "A lot of the people who have not come back to the services on Sunday mornings are older people. Preexisting conditions. I'm not going to fault anybody that doesn't want to come because of that. Myself, I've had heart bypass. I've had cancer. Diabetes. But I still come and wear a mask."

"Why is it so important for you to be here on Sundays?"

Tommy shrugs. "Just to stay in touch with people. And just... hear God's words."

Can you have an epiphany in a church parking lot? It wasn't that I suddenly saw a bright light; rather, I gained unexpected insight into shades of gray. Tommy isn't denying science. He's prioritizing faith. I have to check myself about demonizing true believers as scientifically illiterate.

"I wasn't real smart in school, but when this hit and people started dying right and left, I was smart enough to know... it wasn't fake," he says. "I've been tested one time. I don't know how all of it is in other states, but if you have any kind of surgery now you have to get tested before."

"So you had surgery?"

"Colonoscopy. Five-year plan." He grins. "So I wear my mask—if I go into any store. I know some are mandatory and some aren't. But I'm not going to get bent out of shape if somebody's not wearing a mask. Personally, that's not my business. And I know a lot of people, think, well, we live in America and got all these freedoms, they can do what they want. But I'm going to wear one. Not necessarily for me, but I would hate to give it to someone."

Already along this journey, I've encountered mechanics and shopkeepers and receptionists who haven't bothered to mask up even as a courtesy when a customer walks in, a low bar amid a highly contagious pandemic. And it bothers me immensely. I consider pushing back regarding Tommy's neutrality in the matter, but he's just too darn amiable, so I only mumble, "I worry about giving it to other people, and that's why I feel like other people should be worried about giving it to me."

Tommy shrugs again. "Radical left, radical right, however they wanna do it." Then he adds something that chills me quite a bit. "But you just don't know nowadays. If I walk up to somebody not wearing one, and say, 'Hey, you oughta be wearing a mask. Put it on.' You don't know if he's going to pull a gun on you or something. So I try to mind my own business best I can."

Tommy has me wondering. Millions of people of faith—people like him—are taking at least some health precautions. Thousands of religious services have shifted online. Plenty of scientists identify as true believers. Maybe what looks like widespread rejection of medical expertise only comes from the rhetorical extremes. Could fact vs. faith be an overstated dichotomy?

Well... a couple of days ago, I stopped at a place that would call itself an epicenter of merging academic inquiry and religious conviction. In Lynchburg, Virginia, right about where U.S. 460 has been redesignated the Jerry Falwell Parkway, I encountered a 25,000-seat college football stadium—Home of the Flames. In front of it stood a statue of Sparky the Eagle, holding up one finger, or maybe pointing heavenward. Even the school's motto —"Knowledge Aflame"—gives off a hell-and-damnation vibe.

Liberty University.

I'd picked an interesting time to stop by the world's largest evangelical university, sort of like when the neighbor stops by while you're in a marital squabble. Only a few days earlier, university president Jerry Falwell, Jr. resigned after yet another sex scandal. The university's honor code, called the "Liberty Way," prohibits premarital sex and private interactions between members of the opposite sex. But—oops!—the face of Liberty posted an Instagram photo that showed him with his arm around a woman who is not his wife, their pants unzipped while they partied on a yacht. Then came allegations that Falwell liked to watch his wife getting it on with the pool boy.

Of course, this was long after Falwell resigned his claim to any moral high ground. Just a couple of months earlier, he tweeted his opposition to a statewide mask mandate by posting a picture of a mask showing Virginia's governor in blackface. Which was a couple years after he declared he was proud of Trump's "bold and truthful" statement that there were fine people on both sides of the Charlottesville violence. Which was two years after he discussed the San Bernardino terrorist attack: "If more good people had concealed carry permits, then we could end those Muslims before they walked in." Which was three months after Falwell shrugged off Trump's boasts as a sexual predator, saying Establishment Republicans must have leaked the *Access Hollywood* tape.

After the blackface tweet, 35 Liberty alumni called for Falwell to step down: "You have belittled staff, students and parents, you have defended inappropriate behaviors of politicians, encouraged violence, and disrespected people of other faiths," they wrote. "Your heart is in politics more than Christian academia or ministry."

Falwell's answer: "Jesus got involved in politics."

No surprise, of course, that Falwell would trumpet his uncritical support of Trump. They are cut from the same cloth, faking some sort of piousness while modeling its opposite, claiming folks want a president and not a pastor. But Falwell is only the most egregious version of what will surely rank among American history's strangest bedfellows. Roughly 8 in 10 white evangelicals say they would vote again for Trump— a vile and lawless thug, an admitted sexual assaulter, a pathological liar who paid hush money to hide an affair he had just after his third wife gave birth to his fifth child. Naturally, a great many of them think he was sent by God. It is almost impossible to articulate the hypocrisy and disingenuousness of this marriage of convenience, but Pastor John Pavlovitz managed to do so with passion and eloquence in an open letter to white evangelicals:

"For eight years they watched you relentlessly demonize a Black President; a man faithfully married for 26 years; a doting father and husband without a hint of moral scandal or the slightest whiff of infidelity. They watched you deny his personal faith convictions, argue his birthplace, and assail his character— all without cause or evidence. They saw you brandish Scriptures to malign him and use the laziest of racial stereotypes in criticizing him. And through it all, White Evangelicals—you never once suggested that God placed him where he was, you never publicly offered prayers for him and his family, you never welcomed him to your Christian Universities, you never gave him the benefit of the doubt in any instance, you never spoke of offering him forgiveness or mercy, your evangelists never publicly thanked God for his leadership, your pastors never took to the pulpit to offer solidarity with him, you never made any effort to affirm his humanity or show the love of Jesus to him in any quantifiable measure...

And yet you give carte blanche to a white Republican man so riddled with depravity, so littered with extramarital affairs, so unapologetically vile, with such a vast resume of moral filth—that the mind boggles. And the change in you is unmistakable. It has been an astonishing conversion to behold: a being born again.

With him, you suddenly find religion.

With him, you're now willing to offer full absolution.

With him, all is forgiven without repentance or admission.

With him you're suddenly able to see some invisible, deeply buried heart.

With him, sin has become unimportant, compassion no longer a requirement. With him, you see only Providence.

And White Evangelicals, all those people who have had it with you—they see it all clearly. They recognize the toxic source of your inconsistency. They see that pigmentation and party are your sole deities. They see that you aren't interested in perpetuating the love of God or emulating the heart of Jesus. They see that you aren't burdened to love the least, or to be agents of compassion, or to care for your Muslim, gay, African, female, or poor neighbors as yourself. They see that all you're really interested in doing, is making a God in your own ivory image and demanding that the world bow down to it."

Can I get an amen?

Liberty presented Trump with an honorary degree in May 2017, not long after Trump fired James Comey. "A small group of failed voices, who think they know everything... want to tell everybody else how to live," Trump said in his commencement speech. "But you aren't going to let other people tell you what to believe, especially when you know that you're right."

So I decided to investigate what they may believe. I parked Covfefe in an alternate lot far from the center of campus and hiked into Liberty, exploring what felt like a typical bustling university of 15,000 students. The campus was immaculate. There was a line of students—each standing generally six feet from the other—waiting to pick up their books at the university bookstore. Soccer and football teams were practicing. Guys were playing hoops. I even heard a "bro." Young men zipped around on scooters. When one of them zoomed by on a motorized version, I heard a sardonic "That guy gets all the ladies." To which one of the ladies responded, "Oh yeah. You know how much that turns me on."

Sure, because almost nobody wore protective face coverings outside—and perhaps half inside—one would hardly know that a pandemic was wreaking havoc on college campuses. Yes, the school's academic departments include Biblical Studies, Biblical Worldview, Christian Counseling, Christian Leadership, Church History, Church Ministries, Evangelism, Pastoral Leadership, Religion, Religious Studies, Theology, Worship Music, Worship Studies, and Youth Ministries. And okay, the parking spaces fronting the welcome center had spots "Reserved For Future Champion For Christ." But mostly it felt... rather normal.

At Liberty, you can take Organic Chemistry or Principles of Macroeconomics. You can delve into the Politics of Latin America or East Asian Civilization. You can study Guerilla Filmmaking and Criminology and Shakespeare. There's even an Introduction to Islam. Hell—er, heck—there's a course called Advanced Plumbing.

But I decided to plumb a bit deeper than the course catalog. Tucked between the Center for Music and the Worship Arts and the School of Divinity, I found the Center for Natural Sciences. Up to the second floor. Down the hall. The Center for Creation Studies. And this is where Liberty lost me.

The Center's purpose is to "communicate a robust young-Earth creationist view of Earth history" and equip students to "defend their faith in the creation account in Genesis using science, reason and the Scriptures." As I walked through the displays in Creation Hall. I half-expected to find an animatronic caveman atop a triceratops, but there was actually a collection of fossils—a replica of Xiphactinus, a giant prehistoric fish; a massive Allosaurus skull; two display cases of primate skulls (chimpanzee, orangutan, neanderthalensis, Cro-Magnon, Homo sapien). But the signs surrounding the images told the story. Near the big fish fossil: "Such discoveries indicate that the formation of these fossils and the rocks that contain them were catastrophic events, much as is expected if they were formed during Noah's Flood." Allosaurus? "A large dinosaur from the pre-Flood world." The Cro-Magnons and their cousins? "Our Extended Family From Noah to Today."

It all sounds like objective scientific inquiry. "The post-Flood has long been thought to occur in the Pleistocene in the uppermost layers of the Cenozoic, but recent creationist research has suggested that the transition from the Cretaceous to the Tertiary is a better match to what we would expect from the end of the Flood... Other layers of the Precambrian were probably formed during creation week..." That's some fine geological jargon blended with creationist gobbledygook. The director of the Center for Creation Studies is a geologist. But he's a scriptural geologist. Another term: Young-age creationists. They blend hard evidence and superstition, conflate fact and belief. Fossils and fantasy.

They teach that the Earth is about 6,000 years old. An asteroid didn't extinguish the dinosaurs 65 million years ago; no, dinosaur fossils washed up as a result of Noah's flood a few thousand years ago. Given that most every geologist and astrophysicist—and consistent radioactive dating—estimates Earth's age as a few billion years old, that puts the Liberty model off by... oh, an order of nearly a million. "Not a trivial error," evolutionary biologist Richard Dawkins once said during a speech in Lynchburg. He explained that it's equivalent to believing that the distance from New York to San Francisco is 28 feet.

Knowledge aflame.

The Bible-as-objective-truth crowd would contend that a spiritual geologist and an evolutionary biologist are both scientists with a point of view. Psychologists call it motivated reasoning—essentially confirmation bias on steroids. But I'm a strong believer in the notion that if you scrapped the foundations of both faith and science—erased the tales and discoveries completely—in a couple thousand years, religion would emerge in a vastly different form. But science would develop almost exactly as it was. Facts are stubborn.

Most evangelicals don't think so. A survey conducted earlier this summer, by the American Enterprise Institute, found that majorities of all religious groups believed scientists made judgments based solely on the facts. But not white evangelicals. Fifty-eight percent of them claimed scientists' judgments were likely to be biased.

So Liberty lost me—because they're teaching verifiable falsehoods as possibilities and trying to legitimize the process. As Bill Maher once quipped, "This is a school you flunk out of when you get the answers right." Or to put it another way, if I write this tale of my coast-to-coast expedition with factual intent, but imagine up a wholly fictional chapter about how I spent a day cruising along the Blue Ridge Parkway in an ice cream truck, it would taint the entire account. And the reader would have a right to turn the book into kindling.

Knowledge aflame.

Interpretation of what we see is a product of where we choose to look, what we select as salient, how we construe the facts and form a narrative that fits our sensibilities, our desires, our mood. In fact, the evil geniuses who thought up social media algorithms are as responsible as anyone for our continental divide. I was stunned to find out recently that even Google results vary based on the user's physical location and search history. If both I and my conservative pal in Scottsdale search for "AOC," only one of us is going to be offered positive spins. It's a recipe for echo chambers.

We also interpret facts according to our motivations. In fact, I'll surely be doing this for my entire cross-country journey. As I roam around Science Hill, I could characterize it in myriad ways, using selective description. I might describe how the city limit sign, slightly tilted at a crooked angle, rises from the roadside just before you reach the Science Hill Vapor Shop. Never mind that vape shops are proving to be as ubiquitous as Starbucks during my excursion through rural America. I could simply let the statement leave a hint of sordidness. I could add to that narrative by discussing how I wait out heavy rains—nearly Noah-esque, for a few minutes at least—at a Shell station's side lot. Only when the sun begins to peek out do I discover that I've been sitting in front of an intimidating gold and black clubhouse that announces "Avengers Kentucky." It turns out that The Avengers are one of the most dangerous motorcycle gangs in America. Arson. Assault. Racketeering. Home invasion...

Note to self: Pay attention before you park your house on wheels. Note to reader: This wouldn't be a fair characterization of Science Hill.

Or I could pursue a local story that I stumbled across—about a quilting enthusiast, a widowed mother of four and grand-mother of six named Gwenda Williams. She lives down the road in Somerset, but she was originally from Science Hill. Deeply religious, she attends the Somerset Church of the Nazarene and sings hymns on her Facebook page. Since the COVID-19 pandemic began, she's created thousands of protective cloth masks that she's been donating to churches, police and fire de-partments, hospice employees, Walmart, the Dollar Tree store. "I prayed and ask God to use me and he said SEW," she explained. "Just being obedient to the Lord."

Wouldn't that be a fine way to offer a satisfying stew of deep faith, instinctive charity, and the notion that both can be channeled into practical service and understanding? But my biases are bending me toward cynicism. I fear that, in the big picture, the sort of pious-but-practical middle ground occupied by folks like Tommy Claunch and Gwenda Williams is being overwhelmed by the extremes. So I'll highlight one final tale:

Landon Spradlin was a 66-year-old preacher in Gretna, Virginia, just 40 miles south of Lynchburg. He liked to merge proselytizing with blues guitaring, so in the early days of the pandemic, he and his family drove 900 miles to New Orleans to preach and play at Mardi Gras. On March 13, a few days before leaving, he posted a meme warning that the media was trying to "manipulate your life" by creating "mass hysteria" about COVID-19. Within four days, he was intubated in a North Carolina hospital room. A week later, he was dead.

Spradlin had fervently believed that God can heal anything. "I don't believe there are incurable diseases," he said in a 2016 interview. "There are documented cases of God healing AIDS. God can cause limbs to grow out where they've been chopped off. God can raise the dead." So as he lay in a hospital bed, his network of fellow faith healers around the country began praying for him. They were certain that their Creator was going to cure him, right up to the time He didn't.

But at least there was a lesson to be learned from the unanswered prayers, right? His wife might have begun to understand the risks in overpromising in God's name, in believing that miracles are routine. She might have understood, as doctors and nurses worked round the clock in an effort to save her husband, that while faith is inspiring, science is inexorable. But no. Instead of reassessing her convictions, she rationalized and reimagined.

"I'm not angry. I know who did it," she said. "It's the devil."

Knowledge aflame.

ANOTHER MAN'S TREASURE

SHARPE, KENTUCKY

A couple of days ago, I did something goofy. My route had nudged me toward I-81 for a short stretch in Virginia, the last extended interstate that I'd suffer for a while, probably until Flagstaff. But I pulled off at Exit 54, just north of Atkins, the exit with the big red barn that serves as a restaurant. I know that because it said only, in large letters, "RESTAURANT." I pulled over to the side of the road that weaves toward town, climbed from behind the wheel, and jogged a few steps along a grassy trail leading north. Just a dozen yards or so. I had no time to waste. Covfefe was blocking part of the road.

But I did it. I walked along the Appalachian Trail. Sort of.

Mostly I was thinking of the folks doing it for real, particularly the adventurers trekking the full 2,200 miles from Georgia to Maine's Mount Katahdin. I had hoped to run into a few of them, chat a bit, ask some questions. Were they hiking as a rite of passage? A diversion? Were they simply burning calories? Checking off a bucket list item? Hitting the refresh button? Were they looking for direction amid a directionless time in their lives? Walking toward a better version of themselves over the course of some five million steps? Seeking the ultimate in-the-moment experience?

In almost any capacity, I envied the attempt—the notion of hiking through undisturbed old-growth forests, embracing the unknown around every bend, welcoming the kindness of strangers. And foremost: the escape. Here were some of the headlines from that morning:

**SMALL BUSINESS FAILURES LOOM
AS FEDERAL AID DRIES UP**

**TRUMP WINS ANOTHER DELAY
IN TURNING OVER TAX RETURNS**

**RUSSIA AGAIN TARGETING AMERICANS
WITH DISINFORMATION**

**TRUMP SPREAD MULTIPLE CONSPIRACY
THEORIES ON MONDAY**

WHEN DEMOCRACY DIES IN DAYLIGHT

I envied the thru-hikers, disconnected from tech, seeing none of those stories. At least, that's how I imagined it. The Appalachian Trail actually runs under the interstate for a couple dozen feet in Atkins before continuing on in a more rural-appropriate manner. So below the rush of humanity at 70 miles per hour is everything that feels like its exact opposite. But alas, my chosen mini-section of the trail was lonely. My only companions were a few raindrops and some pesky horseflies.

Today, I find myself in a similar headspace. As I cruise along Highway 68—still called, as far as I know, the Jefferson Davis Highway—I succumb to a western Kentucky version of an ad blitz. Signs have pestered me every five miles, calling me toward the Jefferson Davis Monument, so I acquiesce, mostly because I have to pee. I stop and marvel not at the architecture (the president of the Confederacy was honored with a scaled-down Washington Monument) but at the inscription, an excerpt from a speech by Davis a couple of decades after the Civil War—I'm sorry, the War of the Rebellion. He called on sons and daughters to pass down word of the deeds of their Confederate fathers and that every head be bowed for "all that is grand, all that is glorious, all that is virtuous, all that is honorable and manly." Self-aggrandize much?

This is in Fairview, Kentucky, one of dozens of Fairviews dotting the national map, few of which likely offer much of a vista. Nevada's is a ghost town. Montana's is along a time zone boundary—one block and one hour away from East Fairview, North Dakota. There are six Fairviews in Pennsylvania, four in Indiana, two in New Jersey that are only 15 miles apart. One of Tennessee's several Fairviews boasts that a movie was filmed there—the iconic masterpiece *Ernest Goes to Camp*. And Kentucky's proudly commemorates the birthplace of a fellow who aimed to keep the "servile race" in its place. I'll take Ernest.

But I'm far more interested in the roadside farm market a block away from the monument. The Country Barn and Country Boy Café offers shiny produce, hefty sandwiches, and myriad garden accoutrements, and the entire staff seems to consist of young Amish women dressed in identical white organza prayer caps, not a protective mask to be seen. They're smiley and friendly, and I wonder if the current collective angst has permeated their purposely insular world. Surely, they're aware of COVID-19. Some western Kentucky Amish and Mennonite communities are even hot spots. But they're not scrolling through social media. They're not watching the nightly news. Are they versed in BLM and contact tracing and voter suppression and Trump's latest tweet-vomit? I don't have the courage or crassness to ask. I simply find myself assuming quite a bit and envying even more.

So escapism is on my mind—the fantasy that the weight of the world, which seems heavier than I can ever recall, could somehow be shrugged off or ignored. Of course, that's all but an impossibility for most of us. Every morning, when we scroll through the day's headlines, millions of Americans steel themselves for another shot of incredulity. What now? We're grieving life as we knew it, both practically and existentially. We're struggling to adjust. We don't even know if the Time Before will ever return. So we're seeking uncomplicated pleasures, the comfort of revisiting fond recollections of the Time Way Before. During this global pandemic, there has been an epidemic of nostalgia.

Reminiscing is a behavior; nostalgia is the emotion that is remembered. A few centuries ago, it was believed to be a mental disorder—some sort of inability to live in the present, or at least a sign of depression. The word's Greek roots come from "nostos" (homecoming) and "algo" (ache). Of course, we now know that nostalgia is a coping strategy. It's not that we're unable to live in the present; it's just that, when the day-to-day weather report predicts a storm of uncertainty and cold winds of anxiety, we want the warm fuzzies. Literally, scientists have discovered that nostalgia actually raises the body temperature just a smidge.

I spent much of the summer reconnecting with elementary school friends on social media and Zooming with old college pals. I know of myriad people who have rediscovered dancing, baking bread, coloring, scrapbooking, binge-watching reruns of old TV favorites. Hell, I've been trying to convince my wife to take a deep dive with me into *The Wonder Years*, which would be a nostalgic trip back to a show about nostalgia.

And I just spent nine weeks immersed in the place where my childhood memories are most vivid, a place that feels as if it hasn't changed in 40 years. It's a summer camp in Wisconsin's Northwoods, a touchstone in my family for generations, and it happens to be owned by our close friends, one of whom I met at that very place when we were nine- and ten-year-olds. COVID shuttered the camp for the first time in its 91-year history, leaving a sadness that reverberated over hundreds of people across the country, from age 8 to 80. But our friends, the camp directors, felt they had to be there, if only to manage improvements amid the quiet of 77 acres that are usually bursting with sound. And they invited our family to do the same. Obviously, it was an offer we couldn't refuse.

I then had the luxury of nine weeks of living in nostalgia. I could walk the same routes—and trip over the same pine tree roots—that I had wandered decades earlier. I could wade in the same lake where I'd learned how to swim and fish and paddle a canoe. I could roam from cabin to cabin, locating ancient pictures of myself in various awkward stages. I could glance at the bunk beds and recall with precision where I slept, where I hung my wooden tennis racket, the color of my bedsheets.

I could sit and write half the day while outside my window stood a collection of signposts that has grown over four decades. It began as a means of conveying how a boys' camp in northern Wisconsin had become a place of global scope—nine words

("THIS SHALL BE A PLACE OF WELCOME FOR ALL") repeat-
ed in every language that has been spoken on the grounds. What
began as three panels (French, Spanish, Danish) has evolved
into nearly three-dozen so far. Vietnamese and Portuguese and
Chinese. Hungarian and Italian and Korean. Hebrew and Swahili
and Maori. Arabic and Gaelic and Ojibwa. And then the spirit of
the place came to redefine the collection as a general expression
of diversity and inclusiveness.

    We weren't off the grid, by any means. We still despaired the
daily headlines. In fact, we debated them. The nine of us—a
blended family bubble—would sit down at the big dining room
table most nights and toss around an issue, often stridently. And
each of us was paddling through our own currents of anxiety. It
may not have been utopia—there are no mosquitos in Shangri-
La. But, given the circumstances, it was darn close.

    And yet, even in that near-blissful setting, my old friend and I
still found ourselves talking more than ever about back-in-our-
day versions of the camp experience. The four adults in our fifties
batted around silly recollections of our halcyon days. Feathered
hair. Farrah Fawcett posters. Cousin Oliver. Arnold Horshack.
"Please don't squeeze the Charmin"... "Where's the beef?"... We
were well aware what we were doing—time travel as coping mechanism. When it feels like you're on a dystopian road, it's nice to
take the occasional off ramp.

    So on this sunny afternoon in a corner of Kentucky, I screech
to a halt when I see such an exit. That same Highway 68 has
taken me into Marshall County, just past Calvert City. To my
right, manicured lawns and weeping willows. To my left... holy
hell, how do I describe it? A landfill repurposed into an open-air

gallery. An outlandish outpost in the woods. A forest of artistic absurdity. A hodgepodge of leaning shacks and crooked quips, eerie mannequins and nightmarish murals, discarded waste as works of art, and a painted promise of "Over 3000 Toys and 6 Running Trains."

"Sorry, we're open," says a sign. This is Apple Valley Hillbilly Garden and Toyland.

I park next to a bleating goat and several hogs twisting in the mud, scamper past a few strutting turkeys, and wade into a Fred Sanford acid trip. A semi-trailer decorated with a half-dozen, ten-foot-high, painted clown faces. Trees festooned in carefully arranged debris—hubcaps and toasters and toilet seats—like nightmarish Mr. Potato Heads. Muddy trouser-banners hanging from a slanted roof. A trailer rusting into unrecognizability. Pipework refashioned into sculpture. Piles of tires. Pools of trash.

"Hello?" Silence. A pig snorts in reply.

"Over here!" I squint beyond mounds of beer cans, broken fans, discarded shoes, and corroding fenders, and a long-haired, gray-bearded fellow in his late fifties feverishly waves me over. Keith Holt, who lives here with his wife and kids, is one-part hillbilly, one-part hippie, and six-parts manic. He's giving a tour of the grounds to a young couple from Louisville, pointing to various jumbles of junk rearranged into something resembling folk art. He's a scrapheap artist, a junkyard docent, a prop comedian offering a barrage of truly terrible puns—dad jokes that would make dad roll his eyes. "This was actually my grandparents' working well... It doesn't work too well anymore." Picture your Monday morning garbage collector channeling Andy Warhol and Carrot Top.

"Jack and the Beanstalk" is an automobile jack nailed to a tree painted green. A bike with a push mower for a front wheel is a "Redneck Riding Mower." A gaggle of lounging Goodyears is a "Re-Tire-Ment Home." This is the "Leaning Tire of Pizza." That's the "Valley of Lost Soles." Over there is "Cansas City."

It's not that I groan at the jokes. I wince. It is physically painful. But it's also ostensibly free—no admission aside from a donation jar in a disembodied mannequin hand. Keith remembers being nearly penniless while traveling. He figures broke Americans ought to be able to enjoy something, which seems prescient nowadays. Of course, if he charged per word spoken, he'd be a Beverly Hillbilly. He talks so much and so fast that he tends to jumble his sentences together... because he tends to jumble his thoughts together. I have no doubt that if you climbed inside the brain of Keith Holt—*Being John Malkovich*-style—you'd find a garden full of creative junk and a shed full of mismatched toys.

All of this is actually the residue of broken dreams. Keith returned to his family homestead in 2005—after 20 years trying to make it in L.A. as standup comic, a circus clown, a puppeteer, an actor. He met his wife while both were alien extras on *Star Trek: The Next Generation*. Which seems about right. He brought two truckloads of toys back to Kentucky, along with promised financial backing from some Hollywood pals. He envisioned a large fantasy Toyland—a rideable miniature railroad cruising past fairyland statues salvaged from abandoned amusement parks. But as Keith amassed his collection, his neighbors fumed. They declared him a public nuisance. The law didn't see it that way. Then the county attorney took him to court for failure to obtain an entertainment permit. Keith prevailed again—it's one reason why he doesn't charge admission. But the conflict spooked his backers, who opted out. He altered course. Junk art. Castoff crap as artistic challenge.

But the place is not just a middle finger to the Man. It's a tribute to America and its quirky roadside attractions. In fact, Keith was originally inspired by the miniature village and railway at Pennsylvania's Roadside America. His creations are homages to places like California's Salvation Mountain, New Mexico's Tinkertown Museum, Amarillo's Cadillac Ranch (his version features half-buried lawnmowers), and the various shoe trees and replica Wild West towns that pop up along rural highways. There's even a Stonehenge constructed from toilet bowls.

And it's even more than that. It's also a tribute to his ancestry. Keith's grandfather bought the land back in 1928—a two-room house, an apple orchard, six acres of property. He sold apple cider, probably moonshine, too. When Highway 68 was paved, he added a room for rent and built a small country store called Apple Valley. Over the years, it served as a fruit stand, a four-seat diner, a barbershop, a Gulf gas station. The little building now serves as a quirky museum at the entrance to his property, a nostalgic nod to days gone by—filled with old implements, photo albums, postcards, and 70-year-old receipts. Family lore says Bonnie and Clyde once stayed there. There's a rifle on display that may or may not constitute evidence.

Keith will actually halt his fusillade of gags to tell his family tale, pride in his voice. Just like he'll talk for hours—if visitors will let him—as he guides them through his cringe-tinged walking tour. I, for one, found it all to be strangely spectacular—not because of the product, but rather the effort. Sure, it's an eyesore, as tacky as it is wacky. But it's also a glorious trip into Not Taking Life Too Seriously. If one man's junk is another man's treasure, this is Keith Holt's motherlode.

But I haven't yet seen the pièce de resistance. The tour ends at Toyland.

Keith insists it's a scaled-down version of his dream—that 80 percent of the toys collected from thrift stores and garage sales are still sitting in that semi-trailer adorned with clown faces. But it's hard to imagine more. As he lets me step alone into a shed the size of a walk-in closet, I feel like I'm opening the door into Oz. As my eyes adjust, I'm in a time warp. A mosh pit of pop culture from my past. Countless action figures are staged on three levels, floor to ceiling, packed together as if waiting for a concert from a generation or two ago. Maybe Sister Sledge. Or The Knack. Actually, there's some carnival music playing somewhere, but all I can hear is a cacophony of jingles from my childhood. "I am stuck on Band-Aid..."... "B-O-L-O-G-N-A"... "I'd like to teach the world to sing... in perfect harmony." A life-time ago.

Keith has set up incongruously delightful groupings: Casper the Friendly Ghost hanging out with Hagrid. Erkel rubbing shoulders with Freddy Kruger. Two Jedi fighters alongside Frosty the Snowman. Buzz Lightyear and Woody driving a stage-coach with Laurel and Hardy. Pee Wee Herman riding a bike past Shaggy and the Pillsbury Doughboy. Popeye and Dopey and Ronald McDonald. Captain America and Knight Rider and Jiminy Cricket. The Energizer Bunny and the Swedish Chef and the Grinch.

Toy trains run through the collectibles, each stop sparking an explosion of recollections. There's a Fisher Price Clubhouse! God, I haven't seen that in decades. I used to make up stories—probably my first—about the little people who populated that plastic world. There's a Fonzie lunchbox! I idolized Arthur Fonzarelli. I don't recall any other Halloween costume other than several Octobers of Brylcreem-and-leather-jacket mimicry. Are those the Banana Splits? A rather psychedelic Saturday morning variety show featuring four furry costumed creatures in a rock band. "One banana, two banana, three banana, four..." They were my Teletubbies, if somehow creepier. In fact, recently someone turned the Splits into a horror movie. But can anything tarnish the fictional or frivolous icons of our youth?

There's a Cookie Monster figurine. Once, while researching a magazine article about a woman who writes for Sesame Street, I had the opportunity to step into my childhood by visiting the set. I ran my fingers over Big Bird's massive nest. I peeked into Mr. Hooper's store. I popped my head out of Oscar's trash can. And then I met Cookie Monster—along with the person behind the puppetry, who happens to be the brother of a friend of mine. You would think it would have stripped away the magic, but it didn't. Nothing could discolor my golden memories, not even a guy standing next to me with his arm up a Muppet's ass.

So standing in Toyland was like entering the part of my brain that stores memories of a comparatively angst-free era—a time when my primary concerns were who shot J.R. and whether or not I would unwrap a George Brett rookie card. "Bottom line is, I guess I never grew up," Keith tells me. "I think life's a lot easier that way." So there's E.T. and King Kong and Evel Knievel. The Incredible Hulk and Raggedy Ann and Charlie Brown. Coneheads and Ghostbusters and Pigs in Space. A *Gilligan's Island* playset. An Ewok village. A game of Twister.

Nothing could possibly stain this moment of escape from the gloom-and-doom reality of 2020. I'm reveling in the innocence of... but wait... who's that? That familiar-looking figurine with the long red tie and the pouty expression. The guy posed there, between the Cat in the Hat and Frankenstein, doing that cobra-esque, four-fingered jab that was always accompanied by a contemptuous "You're fired!"

In the nostalgic dance of my wandering mind, the music stops. The record scratches. Oh god no. It can't be.

That man ruins everything

THE HERO'S JOURNEY
METROPOLIS, ILLINOIS

Among the many manifestations for which 2020 will be remembered is an ongoing national epidemic fraught with conflict over profoundly incompatible worldviews. I'm talking, of course, about pedestal-toppling.

In the wake of the killing of George Floyd in May—as systemic racism, already well known to its victims, has finally pushed its way into the general public consciousness—representations of oppression have become targets. As much as anything else, it is an indicator of the clashes snaking through most every facet of American life these days, but I doubt that history will judge it as a distasteful development.

From what I can tell, the movement—symbol-defiling as civil disobedience—seems to have worked. At first, protestors focused on monuments to the Confederacy—not only in places like Montgomery and Greensboro, but also in Pittsburgh, Denver, San Antonio, Seattle. But it has emerged as a global crusade (Montreal, Milan, Brussels, Edinburgh, Glasgow, Cape Town), and it has spurred national self-examination. After decades of shrugging off the obvious imagery, state and local governments

finally have begun to remove Confederate statues from public places—in Richmond and Charleston and Houston and
Little Rock, in Louisville and Jacksonville and Brownsville and
Nashville, in Frankfurt and Owensboro and Decatur and Rocky
Mount. Whatever the reasons—either proactive safety concerns
or not-so-sudden epiphanies—the movement seems only the
latest example of how a little bit of revolution has its place in the
progressive evolution of a just society.

The disingenuously horrified opposition, predictably, has
warned of a slippery slope as broader symbols of historical
oppression have become targets. "Who's next?" they ask. Who
cares? There's a George Washington Park a few blocks from my
house. If I took a stroll one day and discovered that it had been
renamed SpongeBob SquarePants Recreation Area... so what?
Has the talking sea sponge owned slaves? No? I'm good with it.

Trump, with typical nuance and understanding, has con-
demned the activists' actions as part of a "left-wing cultural
revolution" and a mission to "wipe out our history." Amid a desperate need for a national conversation about institutionalized
racism, he simply promises lengthy prison sentences for anyone
who destroys or dismantles one of "our beautiful monuments."
Of course, he is personally responsible for such desecration. A
six-foot-tall depiction of a slave owner is sacred, but Utah's one-
million-acre Grand Staircase Escalante National Monument
apparently is not. Sure, go ahead and bulldoze Indigenous burial
sites within Arizona's Organ Pipe National Monument to con-
struct a wall, but by all means protect memorials to entrenched
white supremacy. Of course, Trump generally shows his cards

with talk of protecting "our heritage." Because what's dogged racism without a dog whistle?

So one side has determined that, after years of being ignored, this form of rebellion is the best means of sparking dialogue about how institutionalized prejudice has venerated figures far too flawed to be celebrated. The other side claims it's not up for discussion. Protecting statues is a proxy for continuing to control the historical narrative. They say it's pointless to fight the past. Battle today's evils. Not only has a statue never hurt anybody, it's part of the cultural landscape—listed on the National Register of Historic Places. In the words of President Myopia, toppling them is erasing history.

But systemic racism is inherently a concept both historical and contemporary. They two are obviously intertwined. And statue defenders are even disingenuous about the history of the statues themselves. It's not only a question of who was venerated, but also when and where. Most were erected during the burgeoning civil rights movements at the turn of the 20th century and in the 1950s—and in places where white residents were eager to justify the continued disenfranchisement of Black citizens. It's the same process that formed and fed the Ku Klux Klan. These statues weren't about commemoration; they were about intimidation.

From time immemorial, statues have been an important propaganda tool—and iconoclasm has long been an opposition device. The folks crying anarchy didn't shed a tear when statues of Lenin and Saddam Hussein were famously toppled. They undoubtedly cheered when photographs showed Iraqis beating the

Saddam statue with their shoes in a reminder of the cathartic power of destroying physical reminders of tyranny. But a monument to secession in defense of slavery is a sacred reminder of our history? Can we bronze hypocrisy?

Maybe the folks lamenting the rope around the neck of Confederate General Jeb Stuart's statue in Richmond should recall that he captured abolitionist John Brown, who was hanged for inciting a slave resurrection. Maybe the Confederate statue found dangling from a street post in Raleigh could evoke the scores of lynchings in the state over the generations. Maybe the bust of New Orleans slave owner John McDonough, yanked down and throw into the Mississippi River, can elicit echoes of the countless unidentified Black victims found in that same river over the course of a century. Maybe, in the nation's capital, the "Black Lives Matter" scribbled at the base of a toppled monument to Massachusetts-born Confederate General Albert Pike—once described as "a bigot with genocidal inclination"—can serve as a substitute for the ubiquitous "Whites Only" nonsense that permeated Pike's adopted South. And maybe the image of George Floyd so creatively projected onto the base of Virginia's Robert E. Lee Monument can remind that "states' rights" was merely a euphemism for the right to perpetuate human bondage—and that each human had a family, a face, a name.

Just a couple of months ago, a Trump executive order proposed a National Garden of American Heroes, featuring statues of the "greatest Americans to ever live." At first glance, the preliminary list of 32 proposed names seemed positively enlightened: Frederick Douglass, Harriet Tubman, Booker T.

Washington, Harriet Beecher Stowe, Jackie Robinson, Lincoln, MLK. The group included a voting rights activist (Susan B. Anthony), a frontline medical worker (Clara Barton), a teacher (Christa McAuliffe), even—gasp!—a professor and president at a liberal arts college (Civil War General Joshua Chamberlain).

But the list-makers revealed their politics, too: Ronald Reagan, but not FDR. Antonin Scalia, but not Thurgood Marshall. Douglas MacArthur, but not Colin Powell. Dig deeper, and the figures chosen seem to reveal a modus operandi. Celebrate toxic masculinity and self-glorification (George Patton). Shrug off anti-Semitism (Billy Graham). Promote unsubstantiated myth over facts (Betsy Ross). And in the midst of a national debate about the mixed legacies of historical figures, the slate of only 32 proposed American Heroes included five men (Washington, Jefferson, Madison, Henry Clay, and a rather obscure Revolutionary War figure named Caesar Rodney) who owned slaves.

Point taken.

Of course, we can erect statues of anyone for any reason. In Omaha, there's a life-sized statue of Chef Boyardee. In Canonsburg, Pennsylvania, a bronzed Perry Como. In Atlantic City, a paean to Mr. Peanut. But for the most part—anthropomorphic legumes aside—a statue is a declaration of cultural priorities. It reflects an agenda. We choose whom to cast in bronze. We choose why and when and where. For the most part, we cast them as heroic. And you can't fake heroism.

Or can you? As I cross the wide expanse of the Ohio River into southernmost Illinois and the little city of Metropolis, the signs keep beckoning me forward: "Huge Superman statue straight ahead."

Metropolis was named not in 1938 (when the first Superman comic appeared), but 99 years earlier—when a local land owner envisioned a settlement along the Ohio River becoming a bustling urban wonder. He imagined a transport center between the industrial centers of the East and the possibilities of the new West. So he chose a name—from the Greek for "mother city"—befitting grand projections. For a time, while the river acted as a superhighway, Metropolis thrived. But once the city was no longer a vital river hub, trade dwindled, factories closed, and the population plateaued. Things looked grim—until Metropolis decided to exploit a coincidence of designation.

The city needed a savior. Why not Superman? For years, the local post office had been receiving letters addressed to the Man of Steel, so city officials conceived a ceremony in which the city "adopted" the Last Son of Krypton. This evolved into a Superman Celebration, a four-day event featuring celebrity guests, costume contests, comic vendors, wrestling matches. The Illinois State Legislature even passed a resolution declaring Metropolis the official "Hometown of Superman."

Then, in the early '70s, an idea was floated—a way to reverse the city's economic slump and give DC Comics the larger-than-life attraction it craved: the Amazing World of Superman. A $50 million theme park featuring a massive Fortress of Solitude with a stained-glass roof, a Voyage to Krypton ride, a Villains Gallery, a Superman Supermarket. A sort of Mighty Mouse version of Disneyland. DC even published a special-edition comic hyping the coming attraction.

The entrance to the park was going to feature a 200-foot-tall statue of Superman, rising nearly twice as high as the Greeks'

Colossus of Rhodes. The latter was one of the Seven Wonders of the Ancient World, collapsing during an earthquake 2,200 years ago. But the former was only an artist's sketch of a dream—and became a casualty of the OPEC oil embargo of 1973. Tourism by car travel was uncertain. Spending $50 million seemed as risky as wearing a cape near a locomotive. The best the city could do was scrap the theme park and erect a fiberglass statue less than one-thirtieth the size of the original reverie. Thanks to some theory-testing vandals, that seven-foot-tall attempt proved not to be bulletproof at all. So the city replaced it with a 15-foot-tall painted bronze version.

I make my way straight for the statue, which stands in front of the Massac County Court House in Superman Square, right along American Way. There he is, hands on his hips in that alpha male pose, muscles rippling, that lock of hair kiss-curled onto his forehead. On this quiet Friday afternoon, a family is taking pictures in front of the statue. The oldest son, all of five, pulls down his protective mask briefly to offer a wide grin.

"Hey, where you'd get that cool Superman mask?" I ask a few seconds later. "Did you buy it here?"

His mom shakes her head. "I made it."

Parents know the power of heroes. So does Metropolis, which clings to Superman much the way Margot Kidder did to Christopher Reeve. Benches in front of the chamber of commerce are painted bright red and blue. The local newspaper isn't the *Daily Planet*, but it's the *Metropolis Planet*. The Super Museum, open seven days a week, brims with "supernirs"—"the largest collection of currently licensed Superman gift items and souvenirs on this planet." In front of it stands a phone booth, of course. A life-sized, fiberglass Superman protrudes from the second floor, as if leaping into action.

A large comic book excerpt covers an entire window of the museum. Clark Kent and Lois Lane are discussing the traumatic events of the day:

Lois: "Don't fret so much, Clark. Now that the information about the president's plane disappearing has been released, I'm sure Superman is trying to locate it right now."

Clark: "I sincerely doubt that, Lois."

Given that this current so-called president accuses the free press of being the enemy of the people, I find myself reading between the lines. But all of the super-accoutrements in Superman Square are secondary to an obvious tweak to the statue itself. From afar, it's not quite noticeable. But from up close, it's jarring. Superman is wearing an oversized protective mask. I'm grateful for the modeling of cautionary behavior, but I'm thinking, *Even the Man of Steel is vulnerable.*

It's as much a slap of reality as anything I've seen, and I find it to be a metaphor for Metropolis, which is undeniably ailing. At its peak, the annual Superman Celebration has drawn as many as 40,000 people to this city of 6,500—an economic impact of nearly $4.5 million. But COVID cancelled this year's version. As I wander through town, I sense a last gasp for the hometown of the Last Son of Krypton.

On Fifth Street, the Massac Theater, an Art Deco historic landmark once proclaimed the "finest in southern Illinois" after it was built in 1938, has been abandoned for decades. Its once-jazzy marquee is stripped to its innards, as if a cyborg has peeled away synthetic skin. Behind a smudged window, a "Save the Massac" poster sits abandoned, too, fallen into crookedness, its edges curled. The theater's last film screening was in 1978: *Superman*.

The parking lot at Harrah's Hotel and Casino, along the river on the south end of town, is half-filled by visitors gambling that blackjack is worth risking a deadly virus. Legalized riverboat gambling has been a lifeline to the community, but the streets are empty. The businesses a block away from the casino are boarded up, including the Americana Hollywood museum. "A MASSIVE TRIBUTE," shouts the sign. "40,000 sq. ft. of America's favorite Hollywood legends!" Huge cutouts and murals of famous faces stare at me, like puppies hoping to be adopted—Marilyn Monroe and Clint Eastwood and Pamela Anderson. Behind a chain link fence and a wrought iron gate—as eerie as a shuttered Wonka factory—more icons wait forlornly. Wax figures of the Blues Brothers play to a soulless crowd. A squat Bob's Big Boy statue holds a double-decker burger, except nobody ordered one. Humphrey Bogart seems about to say, "Here's looking at you, kid." But he's looking only at me.

Just to be sure that the museum has permanently closed, I search online for AmericanaHollywood.com. I expect to see schmaltzy collectibles. Instead, I'm offered only "related" searches that include "How to Vote for Trump." What kind of dystopian rabbit hole have I entered on this journey? I simply cannot escape that supervillain.

Not that he'd cast himself in that role. Trump actually once retweeted an image of himself... as Superman. I'm not making that up. History's jaw will drop at that one. How many mental gears does one have to strip to come up with that meme, let alone shout it about yourself? The retweet retorts were so painfully obvious. Fibs faster than a speeding bullet! More loco than a lo-comotive! Able to build tall buildings in a single con! Shredding the emoluments clause, stiffing contractors, winking at Russian election interference... He's the Man of Steal. More accurately, it may be valid to wonder if we've stepped into the DC Comics story arc in which Lex Luthor becomes president.

Actually, I think maybe I've found Metropolis's problem. Sitting in front of the Hollywood Museum is a huge chunk of kryptonite—a painted green boulder the size of a beanbag chair. The sign says that scientists have "rendered it powerless," that it represents "friendship and good luck to all who touch it." But this is a town with a Uranium Processing Plant that led to doz-ens of deaths from cancer caused by radiation. A decade ago, the operator of the plant pled guilty to releasing radioactive mud throughout the town. Maybe a playful monument to fictional poison is a bit tone deaf. Or tempting fate.

A stunning lack of discernment, of course, is why we're in this mess. Somehow, Trump supporters found a scoundrel and judged him a superhero. They confused the trappings of success with achievement, decisiveness with competence, belligerence with passion, shamelessness with sincerity. Either half this coun-try suffers from a complete inability to gauge character... or they know, and they don't care.

But that's not America's kryptonite. No, our nation's kryp-tonite is its attention span. We fail to learn from history, over and over again, and repeat the same mistakes. We substitute hot takes for depth of inquiry and spread unchecked falsehoods because they bolster our worldview. We filter our information sources into fast-food versions that feed our self-satisfying news bubble. We gasp at the latest stunner spewed from the White House until the next news cycle washes it away, until eventually dysfunction is normalized. We even quickly forget our own expressed attitudes if they don't fit our personal paradigm—hypocrisy be damned. The people who point to the riots proliferating across America and lament that fed-up, disenfranchised citizens can't protest peacefully... are the same lunkheads who told a quietly kneeling Colin Kaepernick to get out of the country if he doesn't like it.

And, as so often happens in a nation distracted by shiny objects, we've lost interest in the real heroes.

If the emergence of the pandemic brought a sliver of a silver lining, it was the realignment of perspective regarding what—and who—is deemed essential. It was truly heartening to see almost daily expressions of gratitude—signs and banners ("Real Heroes Work Here"), sappy commercials, celebrity shout-outs, spontaneous cheers—for nurses and E.R. doctors and first responders. From New York to Nice, good folks clapped from windows and rooftops at the end of hospital shifts. Italians serenaded health care workers from their lockdown balconies. Spaniards banged pots and pans.

Even the adjective itself—"essential workers"—was revelatory. The category broadened as we suddenly noticed the overlooked and underpaid cogs—many of them people of color, toeing the poverty line—who keep the country functioning and allow us to maintain the rhythm of our lives. While much of the world hunkered down at home, some of the nation's lowest-paid workers took some of the highest risks just to keep us from going hungry, from getting sick, from losing contact with loved ones, from being stranded, from dying. Not only the tireless life-savers in medical gear, but also the unglamorous indispensables: hospital technicians, home health aides, assisted living caregivers, pharmacists, phlebotomists, housekeepers, cooks, custodians, cashiers, restaurant servers, warehouse workers, delivery drivers, subway conductors, bike messengers, mail carriers. They simply go to work every day, and we call it the "frontlines," as if they had volunteered for hazardous duty deactivating explosives.

But as the months have passed, it seems like those life lessons about real heroes have faded into lip service. Communal shout-outs have dwindled. Temporary wage increases have ended. Hazard pay has dissolved. None of the relief bills passed by Congress have included protections for essential employees. Nearly 2,400 New York City transit workers tested positive for COVID-19 in just the early weeks of the pandemic. More than five-dozen died. As one train conductor lamented, "They want to call us heroes now, but how can you call us heroes when you didn't give your heroes the proper equipment to fight this?"

Back during London's World War II bombing blackouts, you could be fined for striking a match at night to look for your false teeth. Now people in scrubs are standing as human shields against lockdown protestors. Exasperated parents are accusing overburdened teachers, who don't have the training or resources to craft truly successful online classes, of not meeting heretofore unimagined standards. In fact, teachers have been declared essential workers—not out of gratitude, but to force them back into the classroom, the new frontline.

I have a friend in Wisconsin's Douglas County. She's an art teacher in an elementary school that opted to bring its students back for full-time, five-days-a-week, in-person learning. My friend was given two options this fall:

Choice A: Go to school in a mask, gloves, and a face shield. Push an art cart from classroom to classroom. Sit with a thicket of kids who are only "strongly encouraged" to wear masks and who are not required to quarantine if a classmate tests positive for COVID. Disinfect the whole lot of supplies at the end of the day. Hope that you're not infected. And come home to a husband, in his late fifties, with high-risk diabetes.

Choice B: Refuse to report to work. Lose your job. Lose half your pension.

She's anxious about COVID. She's scared for her husband. She doesn't think it's safe for anybody to be in school at the moment. And she's going to work. Every day. This godforsaken year has taken us to the point when it seems like a luxury not to face constant existential choices.

Meanwhile, I have to make one of my own. I'm running out of food. Covfefe's cupboards are nearly bare. So I drive across town to a Big John grocery store. Remarkably, this will be the first time in six months that I've braved a full-on supermarket.

I'm the kind of guy whose thoughts turn to the worst-case scenario first. Pessimism as psychological protection. On top of that, I tend to internalize the worries of the world. With this global pandemic, that's a recipe for some high anxiety. So I'm quite COVID cautious. This journey that I'm on may seem to bely that. But I'm not flying. I'm not booking hotel rooms. I'm not using public restrooms. I'm not stepping indoors without a mask. I'm not ordering takeout (not yet at least). Of course, the "check engine" light just blinked on—again—in Covfefe, so I'm not sure I can avoid another mechanic.

However, I need to eat. I'm down to a couple of deeply unsatisfying prepackaged meals. So I take a deep breath, strap on my N95, and enter the Big John as if I'm an Allied soldier crossing the Rhine. Seriously. I have to screw up my courage and shrug off existential concerns just to buy some extra sharp cheddar. But I have the luxury of an occasional worry. The grocery clerks do not.

If crises reveal people, it's a dispiriting revelation. Throughout the country, grocery workers—*grocery workers!*—have been subjected to torrents of abuse from deranged dizzards who think they can march in, unmasked, and spew vitriol at the poor guy who has suddenly been tasked with monitoring occupancy, enforcing social distancing, policing masks, and sanitizing store fixtures—all while making $11.50 an hour and no longer being deemed worthy of "hazard" bonuses. Assistant managers are suddenly running security details. Baggers have to be bouncers. Violent altercations become viral videos. Beneath headlines claiming that morale is at an "all-time low," workers are described as overwhelmed and deprioritized. They once again feel expendable. It's a lot easier to praise people than to protect them and pay them fairly. Collectively, our attentions have moved on.

Roughly three-fourths of the folks in the Big John are wearing masks, which means that one-quarter aren't. And half of those people look as if they're checking off every pre-existing condition in the book. Six feet apart doesn't seem to be have registered in most shoppers' cerebellums. I'm dipping and darting, changing direction, like Pac-Man avoiding ghosts.

After racing through the maze of options in record time, I deliver my goods to a young checkout clerk who tugs at her mask, unsmiling, and does her job. Grab, scan, bag. Grab, scan, bag. An occasional "Do you want me to keep this separate?" Grab, scan, bag. She's probably trying to bank money so she can move out of the house. Or she's working hard before starting community college. Or maybe she has a kid at home. I pay as quickly as I can, turn to leave, and then blurt out, rather stupidly, "Thanks for being essential!" She giggles a bit, which is priceless. Or at least, I figure I'm breaking even.

But I'm strangely buoyant as I walk into the bright sunlight of a half-empty parking lot in Metropolis, Illinois. Because sometimes all seems right with the world. There's a statue in front of the Big John—it's Big John, himself, a grocery bagger. He holds a couple of filled bags in one arm; the other, which probably used to hold two more bags, is outstretched, almost like an essential worker version of Christ the Redeemer.

And here's the thing: He's twice as tall as Superman.

DENIGRATION NATION
POCAHONTAS, ARKANSAS

A mind-numbing stretch of Missouri flatlands takes me into northeastern Arkansas. Not long after, where Highway 67 and Highway 211 diverge toward two towns, a sign tells me that "Success" is to the right. I stay left (naturally). So already I have low expectations, and I find myself frowning as I continue west. It doesn't help that Jack Johnson's "Where'd All the Good People Go?" is serenading me forward. Nor does it help my mood that the other town—the one that's not Success—is called Pocahontas.

It's almost impossible to choose the bully-pulpit statement from Donald Trump that has appalled me the most. There is such an embarrassment of embarrassments.

Was it the moment after the Charlottesville white nationalist marches turned violent? "Very fine people on both sides." Was it the time when he stood next to a smirking Vladimir Putin in Helsinki and chose to criticize... America? "The United States has been foolish." Or seconds later, when he said about election meddling, "I have great confidence in my intelligence people, but I will tell you that President Putin was extremely strong and powerful in his denial today." Or, similarly, when he shrugged off the Saudi crown prince likely ordering the murder of a journalist:

"Maybe he did and maybe he didn't." Or how he judged that the Filipino president, who has been criticized for the extrajudicial killings of drug suspects, for doing an "unbelievable job on the drug problem."

I could choose the reference to "American carnage" in his inauguration speech. Or when he visited CIA headquarters the following day, stood in front of a backdrop of the hallowed Memorial Wall commemorating agents killed in the line of duty... and decided to peddle politics. "Probably almost everybody in this room voted for me, but I will not ask you to raise your hands if you did." Or that cabinet meeting comment, right after the resignation of General James Mattis, who risked his life in three wars and spent his career in the armed forces: "What's he done for me?"

There was that stunning moment, after a congressional candidate threw a reporter to the ground for having the temerity to ask about health-care policy, when Trump decided, "Any guy that can do a body slam, he's my kind of—he's my guy." Or when he used sports as another divisive political tool, bragging that he was responsible for NFL owners refusing to sign Colin Kaepernick. "Get that son of a bitch off the field right now. He's fired. He's fired!" Or when he tweeted, "I have the absolute right to pardon myself."

Maybe it's when, during the blossoming of the #MeToo movement, he mocked Dr. Christine Blasey Ford—and her claims of sexual assault—to a crowd of fools in Mississippi. "How did you get home? I don't remember. How'd you get there? I don't remember. Where is the place? I don't remember." Or that time he turned a speech in front of thousands of Boy Scouts into a tangent about hot New York parties back in the day and then added, "As the Scout Law says, 'A scout is trustworthy, loyal... We could use some more loyalty, I will tell you that."

Certainly, I could select his abandonment of accountability for America's COVID debacle and his inability to muster even a picometer of empathy: "It is what it is... I don't take responsibility at all." Or his comments after pulling out of the Paris Agreement on climate change: "One of the problems that a lot of people like myself—we have very high levels of intelligence, but we're not necessarily such believers." Or when he followed a truthful statement ("I have a gut...") with narcissistic nincompoopery ("...and my gut tells me more sometimes than anybody else's brain can ever tell me.")

I could choose his oft-repeated line, including once in front of the United Nations, that "my administration has accomplished more than almost any administration in the history of our country." Wait. Actually, I enjoyed that one—because the U.N. audience literally laughed at him.

But no, there's one moment that most infuriated me—an unexpected choice, but my personal unfavorite because it was a stew of shallowness, childishness, bigotry, misogyny, historical myopia, and brazen xenophobia. It may be the most tone-deaf moment in his four years of disharmony.

In November 2017, four days after Thanksgiving, Trump spoke at a White House ceremony honoring Navajo Code Talkers, who had been recruited by the Marines as communications specialists during World War II. Citizens of 33 Native Nations (not just the Navajo) utilized tribal languages to securely transmit vital information. Within an ethnic group that serves in the military at the highest rate in the nation, they are bona fide heroes. Trump was given a layup. As usual, he missed, badly.

Remarkably—in a moment of either stunning staff incompetence or wicked unsubtlety—he stood in front of a large portrait of Andrew Jackson, his professed hero, the driving force behind the Indian Removal Act and the Trail of Tears. Only a couple of months earlier, *Indian Country Today* had described Jackson as a "genocidal maniac against the Indigenous Peoples" and deserving the "top spot among worst U.S. presidents." By holding the ceremony under Jackson's watchful eye, the administration reinforced that constant conundrum facing observers: Are they more cruel or inept?

And then, surrounded by three of the 13 surviving Code Talkers, one of them a former chairman of the Navajo Nation, Trump said this: "You were here long before any of us were here. Although we have a representative in Congress who they say was here a long time ago. They call her Pocahontas."

There are so many things that bother me about it. The fact that he used one of the proudest moments of these men's lives to reduce them to a caricature, to perpetuate a racial generalization, to diminish a revered historical figure into a derisive slur, to steer a dignified moment into the political sewer, to avoid meaningful appreciation, to reveal his own obliviousness. Unlike the honorees' dialects, Trump's coded language is easily decrypted.

And the cowardice. "They" call her Pocahontas? Who but him? Somewhere deep in that cobweb-filled void where his conscience should be, he recognized that he should probably pretend to distance himself from the bigotry while perpetuating it. So he used passive-aggressive language, as if quoting someone else. It's a subset of his rumor-hawking "people are saying" tactic. Spineless and soulless semantics. For good measure, he then turned to one of the code talkers and said, "But you know what? I like you." Just to add a little patronization to the proceedings.

It was a disturbing moment, but it received scant attention before Americans moved on to the next did-he-really-say-that headline. The episode's lack of traction suggests that racism toward Native Americans has been so systemic for so long—so entrenched, as if the subjugated people are only alive in history books—that it barely registers as an issue. Imagine, for instance, if Trump had a long history of slurring Kamala Harris about some claim regarding slavery in her family history. And let's say he was addressing a gathering to honor the Tuskegee Airmen, the pioneering Black military aviators. And pretend he and his cadre of masterminds decided to have him honor them while speaking directly in front of a painting of Woodrow Wilson, who once lauded "the great Ku Klux Klan." And then, all of a sudden, he turned to the men and said, "You overcame many obstacles. Although we have a representative in Congress who claims the same thing. They call her Kunta Kinte."

Horrifying.

Elizabeth Warren, for her part, has tried to use the kerfuffle as a means of educating. On her official website, she actually has a page that attempts to elucidate: "The story of the real Pocahontas is quite different from the myth that has been twisted by powerful people over the generations. When Pocahontas met John Smith, he was almost 30 years old—and she was about 10 years old. Whatever happened between them, it was no love story. In her teens, Pocahontas was abducted, imprisoned, and held captive. Oral history of the Mattaponi tribe indicates that she was ripped away from her first husband and raped in captivity. When she later married John Rolfe, he paraded her around London to entertain the British and prop up financial investments in the Virginia Company. She was about 21 years old when she died, an ocean apart from her people."

We can be certain that Trump is unaware of the facts about Pocahontas. No, Pocahontas is merely the only native name he knows. He may know, however, that opportunists now sell T-shirts showing his persistent provocateur in a headdress along with words like "Commander in 'Chief' Warren" and "Pocahontas: 1/1024th Indian, 100% idiot." This presidency is a weapon of mass destruction in the wrong hands.

Lincoln once stated, "If you want to test a man's character, give him power." FDR said, "I am neither bitter nor cynical, but I do wish there was less immaturity in political thinking." Truman admitted, "If I want to be great, I have to win the victory over myself... self-discipline." And Kennedy declared, "Forgive your enemies, but never forget their names." And Trump's linguistic legacy is schoolyard taunts.

Let history record the extent to which the most unpresidential of presidents has coarsened public discourse—and has revealed a profound lack of dignity and decency by resorting to slurs against opponents, critics, and journalists that any good parent wouldn't tolerate from a third-grader: Sleepy Joe. Crooked Hillary. Cheatin' Obama. Low Energy Jeb. Crazy Nancy Pelosi. Cryin' Chuck Schumer. Fat Jerry Nadler. Low-IQ Maxine Waters. Little Marco Rubio. Lyin' Ted Cruz. Mini Mike Bloomberg. Sour Don Lemon. Crazy Megyn Kelly. Psycho Joe Scarborough.

Dumb as a Rock Mika Brezezinski. Moonface George Conway. Dummy Beto. Dopey Mark Cuban. Sloppy Michael Moore. Punchy Robert De Niro. Goofball Atheist Penn Jillette. Sleepy Eyes Chuck Todd. Al Frankenstein. Jeff Flakey. Jeff Bozo (Jeff Bezos). Fredo (Chris Cuomo). Mike Wallace Wannabe (Chris Wallace). Alfred E. Neuman (Pete Buttigieg). Oh, and Horseface (Stormy Daniels).

What makes his "Pocahontas" pettiness all the more disturbing—beyond the fact that native observers have complained that it "denigrates her legacy" and is "insulting to all American Indians"—is that he is spitting against the winds of change.

It seems that we've finally reached a tipping point regarding an acknowledgment of systemic racism and its manifestations—at least for all but the most obstinate bigots. Even corporate America began to understand the insidiousness of advertising images rooted in racial stereotypes. The makers of several products vowed to reconsider their branding—Mrs. Buttersworth's syrup, Cream of Wheat cereal, Nestlé's Red Skins and Chicos sweets, Spic and Span. PepsiCo scrapped its Aunt Jemima packaging. Land O'Lakes removed an image of a Native American woman. Eskimo Pie was renamed Edy's Pie. Uncle Ben's became Ben's Originals and removed its logo of an elderly Black man in a bow tie. And yes, even Washington's football team finally addressed the painfully obvious, though more than one thousand high schools around the country still use Native American team names, including nearly four-dozen that call themselves the Redskins.

Not too long ago, I wrote a half-dozen articles about Native American nicknames in sports—a special newspaper section about Braves and Chiefs and Warriors and Indians. I spoke to college athletes with native ancestry and high school principals at schools with such nicknames, the latter claiming they have heard no complaints from their community. But a college professor who teaches a class on racism replied, "There's a general expectation on the part of the dominant group that if something is wrong in terms of race, it's the group being oppressed that has the responsibility to raise questions," he said. "That's part of the problem. The people on the outside are expected to do the questioning, yet they have no power to change it." Institutionalized Racism 101.

I contacted a spokesperson for the team then known as the Redskins, who said, "The name is part of the Washington tradition, just like the Washington Monument." And I found a fan of the team who also happens to be an Akwesasne Mohawk Indian. "If there was a team called the Pittsburgh Popes," he said, "and every time the team scored a touchdown a little bald guy in a white robe threw holy water and waved a cross, how long do you think that would last?" Or, as a chief of the Onandaga Nation put it, "I don't care how you try, you cannot dignify a mascot."

Oops. Did I say I wrote that series not too long ago? I lied. I wrote it three decades ago when I was a sports reporter just out of college. This is not new stuff.

So let's not interpret opportunism as an epiphany. It wasn't an amorphous tipping point two decades into the 21st century that led the Washington Redskins to finally admit the painfully obvious; it was the fact that there was some opposition from FedEx, which has a minority stake in the team and naming rights for its stadium. The Redskins football team battled the

Dallas Cowboys for 60 years. Uncle Ben has been around since the 1940s, and Aunt Jemima for over a century. And c'mon... two decades into the 21st century, a restaurant named Sambo's, for god's sake, finally sees the light? These were mostly preemptions of protest, the same reason why cities started voluntarily removing Confederate statues.

If there has been a national reckoning of sorts, it has been a slog toward enlightenment. But it finally does seem to have arrived. Dixie Beer, a brewery in New Orleans, wanting to avoid any association with slave culture, asked for the public's help in choosing a new name. The Dixie Chicks country music trio renamed themselves the Chicks. The Baseball Writers Association of America voted overwhelmingly to remove the name of former commissioner Kenesaw Mountain Landis, an outspoken defender of the game's color barrier, from its MVP awards.

And yet, Donald Trump, the president of the United States, is still using "Pocahontas" as a punchline. Once again, as with the Confederate flag and the statues, he has chosen to park himself on the wrong side of history. As our nation does some soul searching regarding its mixed legacy and finally begins to understand that every manifestation of systemic racism feeds the problem, he continues to handle the situation with all the grace and insight of a fart machine.

So I can't admit to enthusiastically cruising toward a place called Pocahontas. I fear that something about the place is going to feel... disrespectful—that it might be the municipal version of a stupidly grinning mascot or a crowd doing the Tomahawk Chop. But then I arrive at my destination, and I soon find myself grinning as I wander through town.

I'll shout it from the rooftops: I'm in love with Pocahontas.

I love how a fellow on a riding mower—and I've passed dozens of them—actually waves to me as I coast into town. I love how the first thing I hear upon stepping out of Covfefe in front of Pocahontas City Hall is a distant wind chime. I love how the second thing, from a smiling fellow passing by in a pickup truck, is: "You takin' a picture of the barbershop? Oldest one in Arkansas!" I love how the city's motto is: "Historic. Hospitable. Home."

I love how the marquee of the Church of Christ on Pyburn Street implores, "Live simply. Give generously. Care deeply. Speak kindly." I love how the building that was once the Pocahontas Colored School is now a museum devoted to the history of slavery and civil rights. I love how the old-fashioned three-sided clock hanging in front of the Farmers and Merchants Bank shows that it's 5:08... and 5:58... and 7:20. None are even close to correct.

I love how Pocahontas is home to the Arkansas quilt trail. Dozens of locally-made quilts hang on the sides of the brick buildings around the town square that surrounds a beautifully restored Victorian Italianate courthouse. I love how the little monument in that town square—at the site of the capture of a Confederate general—is sober in its assessment: "Erected in memory of the significant pain and lasting effects suffered by the people of Pocahontas and Randolph County during the Civil War." I love how there's also a sign honoring Sir Henry Morton Stanley—you know, the guy who trekked into east Africa in search of "Dr. Livingston, I presume." Before then, he had been goaded into joining the Confederate Army by "female acquaintances who sent him a box of lady's undergarments to shame him for not having joined up." He was inducted into the 6th

Arkansas Infantry Regiment at Pocahontas, was captured, and earned his freedom by switching sides.

I love how the little local businesses have creative names. Buttercream Bakery. Integrity Tax Services. Visual Eyes Optometry. A nail salon and massage therapist housed in what was an old hotel named simply Ol' Hotel. I love how there's an old-fashioned soda fountain inside Futrell Pharmacy. I love how there's a classy Veterans Walk of Honor in front of the Randolph County Courthouse, but also a meteor the size of a mini-fridge that fell here in July 1859.

I love how there's a Downtown Playhouse a few steps from City Hall where there still hangs a poster from late winter touting a Neil Simon farce called *Rumors*. Neil Simon. In Arkansas. A large sign on the side of the building tells of its previous incarnations, over the decades, as a movie theater, a dinner theater, and a music theater. "We love the entertainment history embraced by the walls within this place," says the sign.

I love how the friendly white-haired lady in front of the Family Dollar gives me directions to Overlook Park—"You want to make like you're going out of town, but when you get to that Japanese restaurant there, take a left..."—and they actually get me there.

I love how Overlook Park offers a Civil War walking trail alongside the languid Black River and how, as I stroll along it, leaves dance from the trees like snowflakes. I love how the city erected a Centennial Wall in 2000 and adorned it with faces that transformed the 20th century. And here, in Arkansas, those faces include Jackie Robinson and Langston Hughes, Jane Addams and Rosa Parks, Thurgood Marshall and Clarence Darrow, Rita Moreno and Louis Armstrong, Wilma Mankiller and Maya Lin.

Sure, there are anomalies. Bill Cosby's on that Century Wall, too. Oops. And there's that imbecile who drove by in a red pickup, waving a Confederate flag. And there's a clueless gas station owner who decided, evidently long ago, to call his establishment Redskin C-Store and Car Wash.

But Pocahontas feels like a breath of fresh air to me, a hint of progressive enlightenment in a part of the country where that has historically been in short supply. Nuance can be a difficult place to find. But this little Arkansas outpost seems to have located a series of sweet spots—between heritage and historical hindsight, between charm and practicality, between art and commerce, between rurality and urbaneness, between appearance and authenticity.

This little city in a corner of Arkansas seems to understand the gravity of its name and the weight of history. In fact, front and center at Overlook Park, is a statue on a pedestal, unmarked but unmistakable, of Pocahontas. Quiet. Respectful. Honoring a revered Native American figure.

HOME IS WHERE YOU HANG YOUR HATE

HARRISON, ARKANSAS

If there were a GIF to capture the evolution of my mood as I drive west from Pocahontas, it would show a slowly fading smile. After a long day of driving through the curves and hills of the flippin' Ozarks, with the flippin' "check engine" light on the whole time, I finally arrive in the city of Mountain Home, only to discover that the flippin' RV park I had aimed for is sold out for Labor Day weekend. So I drive 25 more flippin' miles and spend the night surrounded by the stink and whine of generators from a pack of sleeping semitrucks in a flippin' parking lot of a flippin' Walmart.

Actually, it's the Flippin Walmart. I've wound up in Flippin, Arkansas.

It's rather remarkable how a patch of land originally known as the Barrens could see its name get progressively worse over the years. By about 1850, when it was little more than a flour mill and a general store, the area was known as Goatville. A few decades later, it was named for a local farmer—Thomas H. Flippin. So, the next morning, I can't possibly be the first visitor to roam around puerilely snapping pictures of Flippin High School and Flippin Auto Supply and the Old Flippin City Jail.

The marquee in front of the Flippin Christian Church claims, "You can tell a wise man by what he does not say." But there's no one to talk to. Some 1,300 folks live here, but I see nary a Flippin soul as I wander along Main Street, eerie in its emptiness. A massive American flag droops from a flagpole in front of the Farmers and Merchants Bank, lifeless on a windless day, although a smaller Confederate flag hangs boldly from the porch of a modest house near the Flippin Church of Christ. The Flippin Municipal Building, housing city hall and the police and fire departments, is closed to visitors—partly for the holiday, mostly for the plague.

Last night, outside the Walmart, I wandered the Web in search of anything Flippin and came across a few tales of sordid strangeness from Flippin's underbelly. A couple of decades ago, a fugitive murderer from California tried to hide out here but was apprehended when an anonymous tipster pointed homicide investigators toward this Ozark outpost. About a year before my arrival, a local woman was stopped for having expired tags on her license plate. The officer noticed something unusual in her hair, a small, zip-locked bag with a rubber band around the middle, attached by a bobby pin and made to look like a bow. Inside it: a white, crystal-like substance. Methamphetamine. The woman insisted she knew nothing about it. Someone else must have placed it on her head.

I can imagine more than a few locals over the years have glanced into their rearview mirror and muttered, "Shit. The flippin' police." Because that's literally what used to be stenciled on the side of the police cruisers—"FLIPPIN POLICE"—until some genius finally suggested a change to "POLICE…. City of Flippin."

Surely they grew tired of all the jokes, much like the cops in places like Sandwich (Maine) and Savage (Minnesota) and Peculiar (Missouri).

Then again, the flippin' police: In 2016, Flippin's police chief was demoted as part of a settlement of a civil lawsuit claiming he and other officers had wrongfully arrested a man, pinning a theft on him in an effort to obtain a search warrant. A year later, the former chief was found guilty of felony theft for stealing some $70,000 from the city. As a convicted felon, he can't own a gun, which is certainly ironic. Right across the street from the Flippin Police (next door to a spray tanning salon) stands an empty white building for sale. The sign on the door tells me that this was once a concern known as Ammo Zone. In fact, for a while a couple of years ago Ammo Zone used to be in partnership with the cops. To raise money for the department, the new chief of police would do a Facebook live appearance for a weekly raffle. Lucky winners could choose from a 12-gauge Winchester, a 19x9 mm Glock, a Savage A17 semi-automatic rifle. "It's going to a good cause," he said. "And hopefully you'll win a nice gun out of it."

I'm not sure if I have ever felt so out of my element as I do in this stretch of the Ozark Mountains. I know that mood affects perception, and I've cherry-picked my attentions. I could just as easily focus on the Flippin Farmers' Market or the big Ranger Boats factory on the edge of town or the racial profiling training conducted within the police department. But I've been everywhere, man, and it isn't often that I arrive somewhere and feel... out of sorts, uncomfortable.

Thirty-four miles later, I start to feel a whole lot worse.

I arrive at the south end of the Boone County seat, where a series of billboards leads me into town. Eat at Colton's Steakhouse and Grill. Stop at the KOA Kampground. Visit Mystic Caverns. Meet your State Farm agent, Brian Johnson. And then, like a slap in the face along Highway 65, a billboard stops me cold. The sign shows a gleeful mother, father, daughter, and son. They're holding up an American flag alongside a sketch of a cross, a dove, and a flame. "For the family," it says. It's an advertisement for White Pride Radio and Alt Right TV. There are some 350,000 billboards crowding America's highways, but the signs that have popped up in this particular town over the years—"It's Not Racist to (Love) Your People"... "Anti-Racism is a Code Word for White Genocide"—have managed to pierce through the glut of advertising with a gut punch.

This is Harrison, Arkansas.

The Ozark Mountains can be dadgum beautiful, a hodgepodge of rugged woodlands, limestone bluffs, pristine streams, roaring waterfalls, glades strewn with wildflowers. Mid-20th-century travel writer John Gunther once described Arkansas as "the most untouched" of American states. Also, the "most unawakened." This may be one reason why the region became a haven for the truly ugly. Isolation (breeding distrust), anti-government fervor (feeding cynicism), fundamentalism (seeding apocalyptic notions), and poverty (bleeding into resentment) have stewed into a place that provides cover for radical zealots and hate groups. Separatism. Anti-Semitism. Unremorseful racism. The Christian Identity movement found its footing here, fed by an uber-boob named Gerald Smith, who roused the rabble with spewings about Jews being the seed of Satan. A violent terrorist group called The Covenant, the Sword and the Arm of the Lord stashed guns, grenades and poison gas along the Arkansas-Missouri border. They set fire to a church, bombed a Jewish Community Center, and reportedly targeted the federal building in Oklahoma City before the bombing.

These are not remnants of a fading past. Perhaps the most profound impact of the Black Lives Matter movement has been the awakening of the privileged to the notion that racism is systemic and that the tentacles of that system reach every-where—from law enforcement to language, from education to employment. Institutional, implicit, subconscious racism... it's a massive challenge to tackle. But four years of a bigot-in-chief are a painful reminder that we are not nearly a post-racial society. There are many pockets of the country where it is visceral, explic-it, unapologetic.

This is Harrison, Arkansas.

The Cherokees who settled here were forcibly removed to "Indian Territory" in the 1830s. By the turn of the 20th century, nearly ten percent of Harrison's population was Black, a thriving community along a place called Crooked Creek. But in October 1905, a white mob rampaged through the Black community, shooting out windows, burning down homes, ordering the residents to leave, harassing those who stayed. Four years later, after a Black man was arrested and quickly convicted of raping a white woman, another mob formed, and this was enough to convince the rest of Harrison's Black citizens to escape.

Only one Black townsperson, a woman known as "Aunt Vine," remained, and the written history was similarly vacated. The files of the *Harrison Daily Times* contain conspicuous gaps coinciding with the dates of the race riots. There is scant evidence of any law enforcement intervention amid the lawlessness. It was an Ozark form of ethnic and historical cleansing, surely not uncommon at the time, but still deeply disturbing. Over the ensuing decades, Black Arkansans knew well not to pass through Harrison. It was still a "sundown town." Don't get caught there after dark.

This is Harrison, Arkansas.

Here, in one of only four states without hate crime laws, save one against "interfering with religious worship," white supremacism is something of a city industry. What Hollywood is to film, what Hartford is to insurance, Harrison is to hate.

R.G. Miller, the chair of the Arkansas League of the South, lives in Harrison. That's a neo-Confederate band of knuckle-draggers who hope to achieve what the U.S. Civil War couldn't—Southern secession. They put up a #SECEDE billboard in town a few years back, one of several they've placed throughout the South. At about the same time, on April 11, 2015, LOS hosted an event celebrating the assassination of Abraham Lincoln. A generation ago, one of its founding members told a reporter, "Somebody needs to say a good word for slavery."

Over on Chestnut Street are the offices of Kingdom Identity Ministries, which describes itself as a "politically incorrect Christian Identity outreach ministry to God's chosen race (true Israel, the White, European peoples)." They sell decals that say things like, "Only inferior White women date outside of their race. Be proud of your heritage, don't be a race-mixing Slut." My personal favorite is the link on their website that shows two brainwashed white liberals holding a large-lipped Black baby alongside a cartoonishly big-nosed Jew saying, "Oy. These are good Goyim. They parrot what we teach them on TV and in our movies." That's an impressive amount of revolting bigotry packed into a single image.

And then there are the Knights of the Ku Klux Klan. Check that. The Knights Party—the weakened, factionalized, rebranded version of the hooded archetype, cloaking racism under the guise of civil rights for whites. Thomas Robb took over for David Duke as the Grand Imbecile of the organization in the 1980s. Actually, he calls himself the "National Director" because "Imperial Wizard" is soooo 20th century. Robb surfaces periodically, as the *Arkansas Times* once put it, "like pond scum," from his compound about 17 miles up the road from Harrison.

In the aftermath of President Obama's election in 2008, Robb talked of a "race war... between our people, who I see as the rightful owners and leaders of this great country, and their people, the Blacks." Nine years later, a reporter commented to him, "There's nothing about your message that is mainstream, is there?" His answer: "Well, look at those who voted for Donald Trump in 2016. I think our message is mainstream."

Oh, but it's a family affair. Robb's son, Jason, is an attorney who represents the Klan and likes to talk of "white genocide." Just above the White Pride billboard on the edge of town is an ad for his law firm. It's not a coincidence. Robb's daughter, Rachel Pendergraft has become a pond-scum spokesperson herself. When she's not stuffing herself into a white robe, she likes to dredge up the old saying, "If you think you have trouble with minorities now, just wait until they're the majority." She adds, "I don't hate them. They've got China. They've got Africa. They've got these other countries. Let them have them... We want our own little slice of heaven."

She'd better enjoy heaven while she can, of course, because there's a special place in hell for mothers who nurse their children on hatred and separatism. She has a couple of daughters who are now adults, raising families. But when they were kids themselves, they formed a folk music duo called Heritage Connection. Their mission: "Uniting our race through song." These white nationalist Indigo Girls recorded songs like "Racial Suicide" and "Aryan Warrior." They were still teenagers when they were singing lyrics like "In your eyes burns a dying fire burning long deep within... and our flame is fading faster as our race gets washed away...")

Want worse? Their younger brother, at about the age of eight, hosted his very own talk show—*The Andrew Show*—which presented the Klan's ideology in a format aimed at kids. Still having trouble pronouncing his R's, he started the show with "This show's for all the white kids out there!" and then segued into a complaint about Disney's *The Princess and the Frog*—because the princess was Black and the prince white and "race-mixing is wrong."

This is Harrison, Arkansas.

About a month before my arrival, Rob Bliss, a fellow from L.A. who makes bold statements through video observations, decided to make his way to what he described as "the most racist town in America." He stood next to the White Pride sign and in front of the Harrison Walmart and held up a "BLACK LIVES MATTER" sign. Some people just drove past, one hand on the wheel, the other holding up a middle finger. Others told him he better not be out there after dark. Mostly, it was a parade of insults...

"Have a little pride in your race, brother. White pride worldwide!"... "You're a dumbass!"... "All lives matter, you racist mother fucker!"... "Dude, you're white!"... "You look like a white guy holding a Black Lives Matter sign. What's the deal with that?"... "I'd be ashamed to be a white boy carrying that stupid sign."... "Are you a Marxist?"... "Communist!"... "Domestic terrorist!"... "Explain to me why a coon's life matters."... "Get a real fucking job!"... "Find Jesus!"... "Get your ass out of town. That shit don't mean shit here!"

Two men of different generations walked up to him and then had a genius-level conversation between themselves.

Old racist: "Think you'll say something to him?"

Young bigot: "Yessir."

Old racist: "I am, too."

Young bigot: "Because I'm tired of seeing..." Points to BLM sign. "This right here is the biggest hoax there ever was!"

Old racist (nodding vigorously): "It's the next thing to ISIS."

Young bigot: "It is!"

After which a young woman walked by: "Apparently Black people's lives matter more than us."

One fellow in a Toyota Camry flipped him the bird, drove around, returned, and said, "In about ten minutes, I'm going to be back. You better be fucking gone." An older woman in the passenger seat of a car shouted, "What about white lives? We matter, too! And you're a white man!" Then, as a capper to her classiness, she added, "You kike!" Most priceless amid the barrage of bigoted buffoonery was the lady who shouted from across the street, "Fuck Black lives!" and then added, "And I have Black friends."

This is Harrison, Arkansas.

I make my way to the heart of Harrison, to the town square, where a couple of somber gray slabs near the Boone County Courthouse constitute a Confederate memorial. "This monument perpetuates the memory of those who, true to the instincts of their birth, faithful to the teachings of their fathers, constant in their love for the state, died in the performance of their duty, who have glorified a fallen cause by the simple manhood of their lives... let the stranger who may in future times read this inscription recognize that these were men whom power could not corrupt, whom death could not terrify, whom defeat could not dishonor... "

Ironically, Boone County was organized in 1869, after the Civil War. Harrison was made the county seat and named after the man who platted the town, Marcus LaRue Harrison, a Union officer. Of course, this Confederate memorial wasn't erected in 1869 when the wounds were still raw. Nor was it created in 1899, when the soldiers were still around to be honored. No, it was erected in 1986, just 121 years after an unsuccessful insurrection against the United States in an effort to preserve slavery as an institution.

"Let the Arkansawyer of another generation remember that the state taught them how to live and how to die and that from her broken fortunes she has preserved for her children the priceless treasure of their memories teaching all who may claim the same birthright that truth, courage and patriotism endure forever."

Birthright. Uh-huh. I'm shaking my head at the words when I notice something unnerving—a group of men and some women dressed like militia, armed to the hilt. Many wear bandannas covering their faces. What the hell is going on? Is this a robbery in progress? They all seem to be marching in and out of an insurance agency on the corner. I swallow hard and approach one.

"Hey, would you mind telling me..."

He ignores me, quickens his step, ducks into the building. Instead, he sends out a middle-aged fellow with a mustache that I can see because he's the one member of this faux platoon who is not hiding his face. No face covering at all. Naturally, he stands two feet away from me. Too close. Purposely close. Almost nose to nose. Meanwhile, a giant of a man stands in the window, assault rifle at the ready, staring me down.

I swallow hard again. "Who are you guys?"

"We don't take sides on any form of confirmation, whether it's BLM..." He waves his left hand. "Or whether it's the KKK." He waves his right. "We're constitutionalists. We stand for what the constitution says. We believe everybody has the right to protest, but we do not believe anybody has the right to destroy property or monuments or do bodily harm to anybody."

He says it like it's a manifesto—staccato, self-satisfied, like Tommy Lee Jones in *The Fugitive*, only without an ounce of official authority. Best I can tell, these folks playing soldier are members of the Boone County Citizens Militia.

"That's what we stand for. We are present, but we stand down in all situations and uh... and uh... make sure everybody's safe."

"Here," I say. "In Harrison."

He nods. "We're just makin' sure our town is safe. Period."

"Do you do this often? Every once in a while? On Sundays?"

"We do it when our state and country need us," he says, as if he was handed an engraved invitation. "If it's search and rescue, we do search and rescue. If it's swift water rescue, we do swift water rescue. We do everything."

"Why are you armed?"

"Do you know everything that's going on across the United States?"

"I do... but that's not happening here, is it?"

"We don't want it to happen here. I mean... we don't have to look far."

All the while that hulking figure still stares me down from the window of the insurance agency, like an angry mannequin.

"How many people are in your group?"

"That I will not tell."

"Are they mostly from Harrison? The surrounding area?"

"That I will not tell."

"Is this your office or headquarters here? Why's everyone going into this building?"

He motions down the block. "It's a bunch of buildings and offices."

"But nothing's happening here, and you guys are walking around armed..."

"Second Amendment. It's a free country."

The hulking figure comes outside, stands right beside me, stares some more. He's brooding over me, not two feet away, probably a foot taller than I. A star-spangled bandana covers his face—more bandit than COVID. Dark sunglasses. A hat pulled down low. He lifts the rifle slightly and glares at me.

But I'm not daunted. Heroism is when courage meets circumstance. I'm not going to let some meathead who probably couldn't make it as a mall cop turn me away. Tough talk, of course. My bladder might disagree.

"Is this meant to intimidate?"

"No. Absolutely not." The little guy is doing the talking.

"What's it for, then?"

"Have you seen what's going on in our country?" he asks again.

"I have, but..."

"Okay. That pretty well explains it."

No. No it doesn't, I'm thinking. "But is there anything about this area that gives you fear that it could happen here?"

"Anything can happen anywhere."

I try a different tact. "Well, how do you feel about the reasoning behind what's going on in the country? If you take away the rioting and looting and focus on the protest..."

"I don't have an opinion on that. I'm a constitutionalist. I believe everybody has the right to do what they want."

"And that includes the right to bear arms."

"Exactly."

"And the right to free speech?"

"That is correct."

"Well, what's your take on the state of the nation in general right now?"

"I don't want to get into that. Then I'd have to fall into personal opinion, and I believe everybody has a personal opinion."

"But you don' t mind stating your personal opinion about the Constitution..."

"Yes. I believe what it says, and every bit of it."

Since they're strutting around town, purposely making spectacles of themselves, I figure they wouldn't mind posing for a couple of photos...

"No," says the big guy. It speaks. "We don't want pictures. At all." And then he presses the matter. "You didn't take pictures of our vehicles, did you?"

"What vehicles?"

"Well, you walked down there to the corner."

"Oh, I'm just taking pictures of everything. I'm driving across the country, writing a book about..."

"Well, you went down there and talked to our guys."

What? "I didn't talk to anybody."

The little guy tries to defuse the situation by returning to our conversation. "So we don't have an opinion. We're constitutionalists. And we will not get into a personal conversation."

I turn to the big guy. "I'm wondering why you're worried about whether I took pictures..."

The little guy answers, but not really. "We're neutral. We don't take sides. We're absolutely neutral."

"There's some people out there," says the big guy, "who don't like what we're doing." And I'm thinking, *Duh*. If you feel compelled to hide your face, Klan-like, maybe you understand that what you're doing isn't necessarily palatable.

"We're for everybody," the little guy continued. "We're not against one side or the other. Now, rioting, looting, we're against." He gives a half-smile. The conversation is over. He reaches out a hand.

"Oh, no," I say. "I'm, uh, COVID-cautious." I'm not shaking his hand.

As he's walking away, he says, "All our guys will not give you a personal opinion. They will not address you. So if you see any of our people, they're not going to talk to you. And it's nothing against you. You have the right to the freedom of press. We believe in that one hundred percent. But we are neutral. We don't take sides."

"Okay." I say. I try one more. "You guys going to be here all day?"

"We'll be here as long as we're needed."

So there it is. Manufactured self-importance without invitation. Action without opinion. Intimidation cloaked in anonymity. A claim of preventing conflict, while actually seeking it out. All in a five-minute conversation, albeit the scariest five minutes of my life. I can imagine the discussion once they return inside:

"What did he want?"

"Says he's writing a book."

"A book?"

"It's a thing with pages in it... never mind."

"He was takin' pictures."

"He's in the camper over there—the one with the California plates."

"California, huh?"

"Yup."

"And the license plate frame says, 'Happiness is being a grandma.' That ain't no grandmother."

"That's what they want you to think. Probably Antifa. A spy. Keep your guns ready, boys..."

This is Harrison, Arkansas.

A couple of months before my arrival, in mid-June, that town square was the setting for a remarkable event. A Black Lives Matter rally in Hazard, Kentucky, was an eyebrow raiser. But in Harrison, Arkansas? A stunner. Newspaper accounts mentioned more than a dozen armed men lining the square, waiting for the scene. I'm certain it was the same folks who directed their paranoia at a middle-aged traveler in a borrowed RV. They patrolled the sidewalks. They prepared themselves for a confrontation.

Then a lone Black man appeared.

He was dressed in tactical gear and a military backpack. He carried a shotgun strapped with bullets. Quinn Foster wasn't from Harrison, but as the founder of Ozarks Hate Watch he monitors the state's white nationalist movements, driving around in a pickup truck emblazoned with "Nazi Go Home." As he marched into town, his face showed a mixture of pride and fearlessness, or at least a façade of the latter. Fewer than one percent of the city's 13,000-plus residents are Black. Given the town's history and reputation, given the culture of intimidation and the fact that loud-and-proud racists tend to make their way toward Harrison like cockroaches to a crumb, would it have surprised anyone if this one man was the entirety of the Black Lives Matter rally?

And yet... this is Harrison, too:

When a billboard went up in Harrison in 2013 that read "Anti-Racist is a Code Word for Anti-White," a fellow named Chad Watkins took it upon himself to do something about it: Call it noble vandalism. He painted over "Anti-White," replacing it with

"Love." Somebody called the cops. Watkins pleaded no contest and paid nearly $1300 in fines and restitution. The Klan's Thom Robb later characterized the effort as "hateful conduct." Yep, that's what he said.

Others in the community tried a different tact. They were the members of the Harrison Community Task Force on Race Relations, a multi-racial group of folks sick and tired of having their town tarnished by the reputations and repulsiveness of its worst residents. Said one member of the task force, "If your image is out there that you're this little racist enclave set in the hills, who are you going to attract? You're going to attract racists." So they erected a competing sign: "Love Thy Neighbor." They created a scholarship for minority students—naming it after "Aunt Vine," the lone Black woman to remain after the 1909 riots. They even held a mock funeral to "bury" racism. And, whack-a-mole-style, they've managed to rid the town of most of the offensive privately-owned billboards that pop up.

And this is Harrison: The vitriol directed toward filmmaker Rob Bliss during his stand in front of that White Pride billboard is only part of the story. Although he chose not to include all of them in his video, there were quite a few voices of support while he was filming. Folks offered him Gatorade to beat the heat. They gave him a thumbs up. In fact, the end of the video shows a young woman walking up to Bliss. She hands him a note: "Ignore the haters... you're being peaceful... what you're doing is good... just a friendly reminder... don't give up hope."

And this is also Harrison: That lone figure—gun in hand, pride in place—who walked into the town square for the Black Lives Matter rally was followed by five more protesters... and then twenty. Fifty. One hundred. Two hundred. Three hundred. Most of them were under 30. Almost all of them were white. They marched past the Dollar General store and the *Harrison Daily Times* office and the occasional counter-protester holding a Bible or a poster of an aborted fetus. They moved past the Confederate Memorial, where a sign (erected a decade ago) informs all that "Boone County Men Served Both Armies." The protesters held signs: "I can't breathe!"... Being neutral is not an option."... "Diversity is a code for anti-racism." They chanted: "Black lives matter!"... "Silence equals violence!"... "Not racist is not enough!" And the counter-protesters let them have their day, subdued as if stunned by the scene.

So what is Harrison?

It's a place struggling to overcome a history of profound racial inequality, where pockets of religion have veered into cesspools of despicable delusion, where the embarrassingly ignorant have recently become emboldened by one of their own with a presidential pulpit, and where deplorable people feel at home with their disgraceful views.

And it's also a place where individuals of character are finding their voice via myriad forms of protest, where a new generation is doing its best to lift up the rocks and make the vermin scatter, where courage can outshine cowardice, and where decent people get into what Congressman John Lewis always used to describe as "good trouble, necessary trouble."

Basically, Harrison, Arkansas—the "most racist town in America"—actually represents America in 2020, a place fighting to survive its self-inflicted wounds.

THE AGE OF ACCOUNTABILITY
INDEPENDENCE, KANSAS

E very cross-country traveler seems to come across a subjective dividing line between East and West. I've reached mine. I have driven all of 100 feet across the Kansas state line when I spot a broad-shouldered bison grazing on the side of the highway, as if placed there by a set designer. An hour later, I stop for a rest in Coffeyville, where an entire museum is devoted to the demise of the Dalton Gang—or at least four members who tried to rob a couple of banks simultaneously and were gunned down by the citizenry in 1892. Thirty miles on, I pause again along a lonely county road south of Independence—at a replica of the log cabin known famously as the Little House on the Prairie. It's now a museum built on the site where Laura Ingalls Wilder and her family lived some 150 years ago. They settled on a fertile tract of nearly 5 million acres that represented all that was left of the Osage lands.

Wilder's portrayal of the so-called pioneering life was true to her time, or at least to her memory decades later, but there is no denying the racist language within from many of the characters. In 1998, the book made news when a young resident of Minnesota's Upper Sioux Reservation came home in tears after her third-grade teacher read the novel, featuring natives as warmongers and thieves. "The only good Indian," read the teacher, quoting the book's common refrain, "is a dead Indian."

At about that time, a college professor named Frances Kaye wrote an article for the *Great Plains Quarterly* that echoes this notion: "I honestly cannot read *Little House on the Prairie* as anything other than apology for the 'ethnic cleansing' of the Great Plains," she opined. "That her thought was unremarkable, perhaps even progressive, for the time in which she lived and wrote should not exempt her books from sending up red flags for contemporary critics who believe in diversity, multiculturalism, and human rights." To underscore the point, she called the article "Little Squatter on the Osage Diminished Reserve."

It's why National Book Award winner Louise Erdrich wrote her own series in response to *Little House* titled *The Birchbark House.* So when folks suggest that Wilder's book can be an opportunity to teach critical thinking and to explore complex issues regarding frontier history, the obvious retort is to ask why a current third-grade teacher would choose that book. Its original 1935 description included these eight words: "There were no people. Only Indians lived there."

It was only a couple of years ago, however, that the Association for Library Service to Children voted to change its award for a lasting contribution to children's literature. The former Laura Ingalls Wilder Award is now the Children's Literature Legacy Award. "Wilder's books are a product of her life experiences and perspective as a settler in America's 1800s," said the statement. "Her works reflect dated cultural attitudes toward Indigenous people and people of color that contradict modern acceptance, celebration, and understanding of diverse communities."

Defenders of *Little House* insist that the book is a classic piece of literature that promotes self-reliance, perseverance, even feminism. They say all it requires is a lesson about context along with the text. They veer into what-about-ism. What about *To Kill A Mockingbird?* Or *Huckleberry Finn?* But motivation matters. Which side the protagonist is on—the wrongly accused Black man, the runaway slave—informs the rest of those two novels. But Wilder presented her family as the personification of Manifest Destiny. Unless that is taken into account in an educational setting and taught in a nuanced way, modern perspective judges that as problematic.

So... cancel culture. It's not a new concept, only a hazy new term for it. *New York Times* Op-Ed columnist Ross Douthat defined cancellation as "an attack on someone's employment and reputation by a determined collective of critics, based on an opinion or an action that is alleged to be disgraceful and disqualifying." It's a fine summary, but I would broaden it to include any form of backlash against a person or organization—because those repercussions generate the most controversy these days. Call it what you wish—calling out, public shaming, communal boycott, social or professional ostracism. But the rise of the woke movement on one side, disdain for any form of political correctness on the other side, and social media as a platform for all have made the "cancellation" arena a cultural battleground.

On the one hand, it is decried as forcing ideological conformity, a chill against free speech, a way to shame enough people publicly so that any likeminded thinkers clam up. Two weeks into this summer, *Harper's Magazine* published an open letter signed by more than 150 writers and academics—everyone from Noam Chomsky to Salmon Rushdie to Malcolm Gladwell—that bemoaned "a new set of moral attitudes and political commitments that tend to weaken our norms of open debate and toleration of differences in favor of ideological conformity." While it denounced Trumpian demagoguery, it called for speaking out "against the intolerant climate that has set in on all sides" and insisted that bad ideas can be defeated through "exposure, argument, and persuasion, not by trying to silence or wish them away." This is the crux of conservative grumblings about the "illiberal liberalism" on college campuses.

On the other hand, why the hell should alt-right hatemongers be given a platform out of some distorted notion of equal time? Free speech is a right. A public stage—whether it's a campus lecture hall or an editorial page—on which to spew rhetoric that incites violence, champions bigotry, and wouldn't pass muster on its own merits is not. Nor is strong public condemnation necessarily a threat to that freedom.

On the one hand, conservatives have co-opted criticism of cancel culture, much like they've claimed ownership of God and the flag. They view the Left as constantly moving the goalposts regarding what qualifies as bigoted language and acceptable norms. To some extent, this is most certainly the case. Sometimes it represents progress toward enlightenment; sometimes it's overzealous. Liberals have even begun attacking their own for not voicing vociferous enough agreement or joining in purely symbolic gestures. You didn't post a plain black box on Facebook in support of BLM? Why not?

On the other hand, for conservatives to position it as some sort of liberal invention is laughable. Cancellation as a tool of curtailing free speech has historically and overwhelmingly come from the Right, whether it's McCarthyism translating into the blacklist or comedian Lenny Bruce being arrested for obscenity or CBS cancelling *The Smothers Brothers* because the duo opposed the war in Vietnam or Colin Kaepernick finding himself out of a job. Currently, an anti-LGBTQ organization called One Million Moms—with barely 5,000 Twitter followers—has been calling for a boycott of rainbow-filling Oreos and gender-inclusive Mattel dolls. The people whining about politically correct expectations these days are the same ones who insisted on patriotic correctness following 9/11. Just ask Bill Maher and the Dixie Chicks. And often, their recent shouts of "Cancel culture!" are really just a means of shrugging off sins that they don't deem so harmful.

On the one hand, some view cancel culture as primarily an attack on the well-known. A celebrity shares a controversial opinion or exhibits abhorrent behavior and either survives the storm in the public domain (J.K. Rowling, Dave Chappelle, maybe Woody Allen), doesn't seem to at all (Don Imus, Roseanne Barr, Kevin Spacey), or is relegated to purgatory while consumers and corporate America reconsider second chances (Mel Gibson, Tiger Woods, Louis C.K.).

On the other hand, you don't have to be famous to be permanently marked. In an era when most everyone has an iPhone and social media accounts, one racist rant caught on video or one late-night comment on Twitter can permanently mark someone as a "Karen" these days. Granted, usually they've stepped it in themselves.

On the one hand, cancellation can be a very personal judgment. I'm friendly with a guy who proudly wears an "Italians for Trump" shirt. He long idolized Robert De Niro, even hung a poster of him in his den—until De Niro started excoriating Donald. The guy took the poster down and made a point of posting a Facebook photo of him doing so. Priorities declared.

On the other hand, cancellation can be as public as broad calls to boycott. Liberals—myself included—stay away from Chick-Fil-A and Hobby Lobby. Conservatives rail against Nike and the NBA. Trump, a man who cancels every contradictory opinion within his own administration, stood in front of Mount Rushmore and declared that cancel culture is a political weapon "demanding total submission from anyone who disagrees. This is the very definition of totalitarianism." Six weeks later, he urged consumers to snub Goodyear tires, claiming that the company had banned MAGA hats. Just like he urged boycotts of AT&T before that. And Harley-Davidson. And Apple. And Macy's. And he called for the firing of *Meet the Press* anchor Chuck Todd. And *New York Times* columnist Paul Krugman. And Fox News commentator Charles Krauthammer. And actress Debra Messing. And on and on and on.

On the one hand, cancel culture is very much a product of the current zeitgeist. It is a hot take as a verdict. A little over a decade ago, a Texas school district chose to provide to each student one of my children's books—about sport's greatest moments.

The only problem: The cover of the book, one of my favorites, featured Michael Phelps, who had been photographed with a bong only a few months earlier. Pretty tame in retrospect. Barely a scandal. But the PTA in Texas made a big ask: Could the publisher print 1,500 new book jackets, sans Phelps? To my surprise, that's what happened. The new Waco-only cover included... wait for it... Lance Armstrong. Timing is everything.

On the other hand, people in positions of power are being judged on something they did decades earlier, whether it's Justice Brett Kavanaugh and sexual assault or Governor Ralph Northam and blackface. Often, cancellation becomes a matter of I-know-it-when-I-see-it through a lens of contemporary sensibilities. That also encompasses historical icons, whether it's Confederate generals, team mascots, or that little house on the Kansas prairie.

Which brings me to Oz. Kansas is where *The Wonderful Wizard of Oz*, the classic book by L. Frank Baum that became the iconic film, comes to life—or at least tries to in various places. In Marego, Kansas, there's a Wizard of Oz Museum, an Oz Winery, and an annual OZtoberfest. There are Yellow Brick Roads in Wichita and Sedan. The city of Liberal—where I'll be headed in a couple of days—is home to Dorothy's House and the Land of Oz. Last year, the Kansas State Fair exhibited a sculpture of Dorothy and her crew made out of 1,200 pounds of butter. If you stop seeing Oz references, you know you're not in Kansas anymore.

Given the state's total embrace of the tale, it is ironic—to say the least—that Baum never actually lived in Kansas. He had been there only once, in 1882, when he and his new bride Maud were on a multi-state tour to promote a melodrama he wrote. They visited a couple of cities over a couple of days and never returned. "I don't think much of Kansas," Maud wrote to her family. "I couldn't be paid to live here." So when Baum, who wrote the book in Chicago, describes "nothing but the great gray prairie on every side" and the land plowed into "a gray mass" and the grass "the same gray color to be seen everywhere" and a house "as dull and gray as everything else," he may have been offering judgment as much as painting a picture.

Baum published the book in 1900. Over the next several decades, many libraries across the country banned it—in Chicago, Detroit, even in Kansas City. As late as 1986, several fundamentalist Christian families in Tennessee filed a lawsuit objecting to the book's inclusion in a public school's syllabus. The reasons ran the gamut: Fantasy stories are unhealthy for children. Good witches are theologically impossible. The female main character was too strong. Oz is a communist state. But these absurd reasons obscured what should have been the obvious one: L. Frank Baum was horribly racist.

Here are three lines that Baum wrote in *The Wonderful Wizard of Oz*: "Some people without brains do an awful lot of talking, don't you think?"… "If you only knew it, you are in luck not to have a heart."… "It is such an uncomfortable feeling to know one is a fool."

And this is what Baum wrote as editor of a South Dakota newspaper, the *Aberdeen Pioneer*, on December 20, 1890: "The proud spirit of the original owners of these vast prairies inherited through centuries of fierce and bloody wars for their possession, lingered last in the bosom of Sitting Bull. With his fall the nobility of the Redskin is extinguished, and what few are left are a pack of whining curs who lick the hand that smites them. The Whites, by law of conquest, by justice of civilization, are masters of the American continent, and the best safety of the frontier settlements will be secured by the total annihilation of the few remaining Indians. Why not annihilation? Their glory has fled, their spirits broken, their manhood effaced; better that they die than live as the miserable wretches that they are."

Total annihilation. Extermination. Nine days later, near Wounded Knee Creek in South Dakota, a detachment of the U.S. 7th Cavalry Regiment massacred more than 250 Lakota men, women, and children. Women shot with infants in their arms. Little boys surrounded and butchered. Mothers and children ferreted out from caves and murdered. Twenty of the soldiers were awarded the medal of honor. It wasn't until a century later that both houses of Congress passed a resolution expressing "deep regret."

And here's what L. Frank Baum wrote five days after the carnage at Wounded Knee: "The *Pioneer* has before declared that our only safety depends upon the total extermination of the Indians. Having wronged them for centuries we had better, in order to protect our civilization, follow it up by one more wrong and wipe these untamed and untamable creatures from the face of the earth."

When Baum's views made news a few decades ago, a woman from the South Dakota Historical Society shrugged it off. She said, "He didn't spend much ink on the subject. It was not a deeply felt conviction. I don't think it was a big side of Baum." Right. Just a casual incitement to genocide.

Baum was certainly an enigma. His book was a bestseller for two years, but he wound up filing for bankruptcy. He was a suffragist, yet he espoused subjugation. His utopian merry old land of Oz came from the same mind that produced children's poems with titles like "There Was a Little N----- Boy." He wrote another tale in which he described the "wicked" Awgwas tribe as "a transient race, passing from life into nothingness." Of course, Baum thought enough of himself to claim divine inspiration for his stories, a positively Trumpian spin: "Sometimes the Great Author has a message to get across and He has to use the instrument at hand. I happened to be that medium, and I believe the magic key was given me to open the doors to sympathy and understanding, joy, peace and happiness."

But in 2006, more than a century after Baum wrote about lions and tigers and bears and genocide, two of Baum's descendants traveled to South Dakota to address a gathering of Sioux from reservations in the state. Their statement was a horse of a different color. "We're here to say that we're sorry," said Baum's great-great-grandson, "and to acknowledge these calls to genocide that culminated in a bloody massacre like Wounded Knee." Added Baum's great-granddaughter, simply, "We felt called to make a connection with the descendants' survivors." Sometimes it's just about owning up to the ugly.

So on the one hand, a call for cancellation might focus on the message, such as Laura Ingalls Wilder's portrayal of frontier life. But on the other hand, what do you do with a beloved product from a terribly flawed producer? Michael Jackson played the Scarecrow in *The Wiz*. And Michael Jackson was almost certainly a pedophile. Some radio stations pulled his songs. *The Simpsons* even pulled an episode featuring his voice. But millions still love listening to his music. It is a cultural conundrum.

It may be that the best generalization about cancel culture is that it shouldn't be generalized. It isn't always about liberal sensitivity, or egregious and extreme commentary, or the proletariat attacking the powerful and famous. It isn't even always about moral outrage. Sometimes, cancellation (in a manner of speaking) is undoubtedly merited—not all views are equal; some are worthy of public scorn and consequence. But sometimes, the moral failure is on the part of the would-be cancellers.

I speak from experience. I was one of the first people to actually lose a job because of Trump. Sort of. Back in the spring of 2016, when it became evident that he was going to be the Republican nominee for president, my wife and I hoped to stave off the unthinkable while trying to find a creative way to express the courage of our convictions. Amy was taking art classes; I'm a writer. Many of my published books are alphabet picture books for kids. So we decided to collaborate on an adult parody version. We called it *D is for Dump Trump: An Anti-Hate Alphabet.*

It was seriously funny, earnestly tongue-in-cheek. Amy drew a bunch of editorial cartoons, and I wrote 26 poems about the dangers of Donald Trump. L was for lying, M was for misogyny, N was for narcissism, and so on. It was the easiest ABC book I've ever written. Usually, I get stymied by the letter X, for instance. Thank you, President Xenophobia.

We launched a little Kickstarter campaign, our primary goal being to print and disseminate the book to Democratic campaign workers, while also donating proceeds to the Southern Poverty Law Center, which tracks and fights hate groups throughout the country. Success was unlikely. The whole project was a blip on the public consciousness—roughly the equivalent of putting up a sign in our front yard amid the white noise of millions of voices doing much the same.

But then we got fired.

For 16 years, ever since my first travel memoir led to some high-profile TV interviews, we had served as spokespeople for... well, an industry that is currently rolling during the pandemic. Let's just say that when I opted to set foot in a house-on-wheels again, it was evidence that hell had indeed frozen over. For more than a decade and a half, we devoted our summers to traveling around a segment of the country and appearing on regional morning news shows. Always, we talked about the journey we were on and the joys of seeing the country one mile at a time. We would spend months planning the tour and contacting scores of TV producers. It was our main focus—and accounted for roughly two-thirds of our annual income.

When the Kickstarter campaign began, we were well into our 17th summer tour, having already done interviews in L.A., San Diego, Tucson, Phoenix—all on point. None of my books, not even my travel memoirs, were mentioned. Certainly, we wouldn't have dared discuss anything political during those TV appearances. That would be cause for termination.

But we made one mistake. One fellow on our contact list turned out to be a Trump supporter with an ax to grind against the folks who hired us. He apparently forwarded our Kickstarter video to a fellow Trumper who published an industry newsletter. Within two hours, this sanctimonious hack had posted an incendiary and completely unresearched column. He described our "wildly popular" book (it had exactly 18 Kickstarter backers at the time and wasn't even for sale during the summer). He suggested, shamefully, that we were going to use our platform to promote our politics. Then he veered into an absurd hypothetical—that we might somehow be ambushed in an interview and forced to discuss the election. Really? By people whose preparation consisted of glancing at our press release for the first time as they rushed out to do a three-minute puff piece? Usually, we had to remind them of our names. Once, during a five-minute interview in Chicago, I was called "Dave" the whole time. But apparently, there was great fear that a morning meteorologist on *Good Day, Fresno* was going to morph into Mike Wallace.

It was all, quite literally, fake news. But one part was very real: He called for the industry to terminate its relationship with "these California liberals" who "need other people's money to publish a book." And within 24 hours, that's exactly what happened.

There was little regard for loyalty or truth; it was simply a move to avoid bad publicity. Toward that end, the decision was as shortsighted as it was spineless because it profoundly pissed us off. So we decided to go public about it. It emerged as national news, even international. Nearly one thousand people from all over the world contributed to our Kickstarter campaign.

But of course, we lost our beloved jobs. And we suffered through a smattering of hate mail, along with gobs of online anonymity utilizing the full array of Trumper depth of thought ("they look like an inbred family"). You can imagine how we felt when election night didn't offer karmic reward. And, of course, these past four years have been even lower than the lowest of expectations. But mostly, I'm glad that it happened. The response to our little cartoon book turned out to be far more important than the book itself. We were able to pull back the curtain—Toto-like—to expose the true colors of our employers. We were provided a much larger platform from which to make our case and become a fleeting addition to a tiny part of the 2016 election narrative. And I remain immensely proud of our efforts, now recorded for posterity. No regrets. Zero.

So as I pass the geographical midway point of my cross-country journey, I recognize that there are layers to the trip I'm taking beyond the desire to chronicle this specific moment. I may be seeking some form of redemption, a life raft of optimism, a sense that the country's moral compass could point north again, an indication that there's something hopeful somewhere over some sort of rainbow.

Baum's tin man discovered that he had a heart all along. I'm hopeful my country will, too.

WINDS OF CHANGE

GREENSBURG, KANSAS

The drive west through Kansas is a physical struggle. Over several hundred miles, Covfefe and I fight the wind sweepin' down the plain—or rather, up from Oklahoma. My muscles are actually hurting from battling the southerly breeze, but at least it livens up the drive. Kansas can be a treadmill of an experience, miles of sameness interrupted by an occasional shrug. Grain elevators—prairie skyscrapers—rise every few dozen miles, visible from a distance as exclamation points amid what feels like one long sentence. So it can be tempting, during a yawning stretch of highway, to snicker at a billboard beckoning travelers to "the world's largest hand-dug well" in the town of Greensburg. My thoughts turn to Chevy Chase in *Vacation*, trying to motivate his family to see "the second largest ball of twine on the face of the earth... only four short hours away."

The largest ball of twine? It's in Cawker City, Kansas.

Of course, I can't blame the state for mining for superlatives. I admire the effort. My route to Greensburg has taken me through Coffeyville's brag about gunning down bank robbers, and Dexter's boast about lifting up ("Where Helium Was Invented"), and Pratt's preening about hosting the annual Miss

Kansas pageant ("Home of the Beautiful Women"). Not too far from here, the city of Manhattan calls itself "The Little Apple," and in the tiny town of Gas, a bright red water tower announces simply, GAS KAN. The town's slogan: "Don't pass gas. Stop and enjoy it!"

How often is it that you can rumble along a rural highway, languidly turn your eyes to a billboard on the side of the road... and burst out laughing? Well, a good number of rural hiccups have learned not to take themselves too seriously. When attempting to make their mark on the memories of passersby, they've discovered the power of self-deprecation.

In fact, in a couple of days I'll be passing through one of my favorites—Hooker, Oklahoma. It was named after a local ranch foreman named John "Hooker" Threlkeld. I'm not making that up—Hooker was named for a guy named John. Frankly, not unlike Flippin, most everything about Hooker gives me the giggles, something too infrequent in my world these days. Immature? You bet. But in the words of Walt Whitman, "I am large; I contain multitudes." One of them is a juvenile sense of humor. Of course, Hooker seems to have one, too. There used to be a welcome sign at the edge of town that included an image of a 19th-century prostitute. The newspaper is called the *Hooker Advance*. There's a Hooker True Value hardware store. The local American Legion baseball team is the Hooker Horny Toads. And the town slogan would make Mark Twain grin: "It's a location, not a vocation."

In my travels, I have collected town slogans like so many refrigerator magnets. It's a tall order to describe yourself in half-a-dozen words and then imprint the phrase on all who encounter it, especially for places that are a bit short on uniqueness. For instance, I don't remember much about the time, many years back, when I passed through Gettysburg, South Dakota. In fact, nothing at all—except the delightful sign: "Gettysburg, South Dakota. Where the Battle Wasn't."

Town slogans run the gamut from clever (Garden City, Missouri: "A Touch of Heaven on Highway Seven") to hyperbolic ("Welcome to the only Eaton Rapids on Earth") to hysterically desperate (Forest Junction, Wisconsin: "You Can Get There From Here"). But they all have one thing in common: A slogan identifies a community as a place of some import, a destination worthy of consideration.

I would argue, in fact, that much of the conflict sweeping through America at this moment is a product of that all-too-human need for attention, for a voice. Myriad Americans feel passed by like a blur on the side of an interstate, relegated to a state of insignificance—culturally, politically, financially, humanely—whether we're talking about Black lives or refugee families or subsistence farmers or small business owners or transgender students or overworked teachers or underappreciated health care workers.

Or Trump supporters. The common refrain about 2016 Trump voters was that they felt ignored by those governing, dismissed by career politicians. I believe it's a too-sunny rationalization for what were often darker impulses. Their continued support amid his pathological parade suggests so. But still, the notion remains. America is immersed in a collective identity crisis, a search for acknowledgment. So we find catharsis in protests or rallies, in extremism on both sides, in conspiracy theory, in tabloid fame, in social media run amuck. We traffic in hyperbole. We rattle the cage. We say, "That got your attention," and it somehow confirms our existence.

So communities do it, too. How do thousands of towns make their mark, especially when their target audience is speeding by at 70 miles per hour? Most any community can bill itself as the Whatzit City, or the Birthplace of the Thingamajiggy, or the Hometown of Whomever. The most common means of forging an identity seems to be by calling oneself the Something Capital of the Someplace, in which case its merely a matter of how high to aim. Consider three communities in Wisconsin: Sauk City is the "Cow Chip Throwing Capital of Wisconsin," and Reedsburg is the "Butter Capital of America." But Green Bay is the "Toilet Paper Capital of the World."

Often, a town's identity is all about location, location, location. If it's on the edge of something, it's a gateway (Bolivar, Ohio: "Gateway to Tuscanawas County"). If it's at the confluence of roads or rivers or regions, it's either a magical meeting (Lowry City, Missouri: "Where the Ozarks Meet the Plains") or a proud crossroads (Barstow, California: "Crossroads of Opportunity"). And if it is centrally located, then it's vying to be the center of our attention—the center of the state, the middle of the country, or (bless you, Boswell, Indiana) the "Hub of the Universe."

Granted, some towns try to fit too much into a slogan (Bangor, Michigan: "Train City USA in the Heart of Apple Country". Or perhaps not enough (Little Valley, New York: "A Municipal Electric Community"). But a little imagination goes a long way. I particularly appreciate the warm-hearted generalities substituting for specifics. When Wasko, California, announces that it's "A Nice Place to Live," I have no reason to doubt it. Same goes for

Pigeon Falls, Wisconsin: "Where Everyone is Important." And Canfield, Ohio, is "The City That Cares."

Given all that there is to choose from, whittling the wit and whimsy down to a list of favorites has been a challenge. But I've managed to come up with my Top 20:

- Newton Falls, Ohio: The town with zip
- Gettysburg, South Dakota: Where the battle wasn't
- Hooker, Oklahoma: It's a location, not a vocation
- Boswell, Indiana: Hub of the universe
- Jewell, Iowa: A gem in a friendly setting
- San Andreas, California: It's not our fault
- Moscow, Maine: Best town by a dam site
- Peculiar, Missouri: Where the odds are with you
- Linesville, Pennsylvania: Where the ducks walk on the fish
- Union Springs, Alabama: Serendipity center of the South
- Apex, North Carolina: The peak of good living
- Hereford, Texas: Town without a toothache
- Rockwell City, Iowa: The golden buckle on the Corn Belt
- Walla Walla, Washington: The city so nice they named it twice
- Freeland, Pennsylvania: The most happening place on Earth
- Gretna, Virginia: Ain't no big thing, but we're growing!
- Spring Lake, Michigan: Where nature smiles for seven miles
- Morrison, Colorado: The nearest faraway place
- Beaver Dam, Wisconsin: Make yourself at home
- Gravity, Iowa: We're down to earth

Of course, there is a tremendous difference between acknowledgment and effect. Passersby may grin, but would the sign make them stop in Garden City or Eaton Rapids or Union Springs? Probably not. And in this time of COVID-19, when stopping anywhere is an existential decision, these blips along the highways—which would love the extra tax revenue brought in by travelers and curiosity seekers—are generally afterthoughts. So I probably won't even stop in Hooker—a location, but not my destination.

But Greensburg? Well, Greensburg actually has something to boast about.

On May 4, 2007, a massive EF5 tornado—nearly two miles wide and reaching winds of 205 miles per hour—leveled the town. Complete devastation. Some 95 percent of the homes and businesses in Greensburg were destroyed. The rest were severely damaged. Only three structures were left standing, including the grain elevator. Eleven people died, and hundreds of people lost nearly everything they owned. In 65 minutes, a 122-year-old town of more than 1,500 souls had essentially disappeared.

The residents could have let the city complete its death throes and moved to neighboring towns—and, indeed, it remains about half as populous as it was before that mid-spring nightmare. But here's how they reacted in Greensburg: "Although this storm was devastating to our community, we are presented with an incredible opportunity to show the world our strength and to create a new future for those who will live here. We are rebuilding stronger, better, greener, and we are a model for rural America."

These are the words on the other billboard on the outskirts of Greensburg: "Rebuilding Stronger, Better, Greener."

You wouldn't necessarily know it while speeding past town, maybe en route to Dodge City 45 miles away. But, as the U.S.

Department of Energy put it, Greensburg—which is actually named for a 19th-century stagecoach driver named D.R. "Cannonball" Green—serves as "a national model for green communities." LED streetlights. Family homes adopting energy-efficient building codes. Distributed renewable energy. An art center powered by solar panels and wind turbines. Wood siding made from reclaimed lumber. The most LEED certified buildings per capita, they claim, in the world. A year after the tornado, George W. Bush became the first president ever to give a high school commencement address, telling the Greensburg High class of 2008, "The leaders of your town understand that out of the devastation of the storm comes an opportunity to rebuild with a free hand and a clean slate."

I pull into an RV park in Greensburg—really just a parking lot of a cheap motel—and Covfefe wheezes to a stop, still struggling for breath every time I come to a halt. It can be exhausting trying to time when to start coasting toward a stoplight, hoping it turns green before the engine dies. Maybe it's the heavy air. It's stiflingly hot, nearly triple digits. As I climb out, a forever freight train arrives, rumbling by no more than 200 feet away. Everything feels interminable at the moment—the heat, the wind, the sound of one double-stacked car after another passing by. As I take a short walk into town, I welcome the cooling effect of the stiff breeze. For now.

I want to see the Big Well. Created in 1887, it was an engineering marvel in its day—109 feet deep and 32 feet in diameter. When the tornado arrived, the building constructed over the well was destroyed, along with its water tower. Only the well remained, which you can descend via a dramatic spiral staircase. But the museum and visitor center surrounding it has been reconstructed into a series of exhibits about the history of Greensburg and the tornado's destruction (everything from twister-strewn refuse behind glass to real-time weather reports). All of it is housed in a building with a spiral motif, as if approximating the shape of a twister. It is truly, unexpectedly inspiring.

A few blocks away, at the Twilight Theater, the proprietor is removing the lettering of last week's movie from the marquee. I can Wheel-of-Fortune it enough to figure out that it used to say "Dora and the Lost City of Gold," though I happen to walk by when it's mostly just "Lost City." But the Big Well Museum is a monument to a town's refusal to lose its life. Nearby, across from City Hall, an outdoor sculpture features a passage from the Book of Isaiah: "Some of you will rebuild the deserted ruins of your city. Then you will be known as a rebuilder of walls and a restorer of homes." It turns out that a stop in Greensburg is a lesson in humility, fortitude, and community. If only we could supersize it.

Maybe we should. Greensburg's rise from the ruins was the result of an unplanned paradigm shift, and maybe that's where we find ourselves now. Donald Trump was a blind experiment on the part of millions of Americans. They wanted to shake up the system. No, blow it up. *We're tired of everyone drinking the Obama Kool-Aid,* they said. *Let's all drink bleach.* What could possibly go wrong? Well... not just the worst president, but arguably the worst possible president.

I wrote a movie screenplay about a decade ago, when Trump was just a racist birther blowhard, in which I suggested that reincarnation was a reality. "Trump," said one all-knowing character, "used to be a slug." Turns out I was too kind. Trump has swept through the American landscape like an EF5 tornado, dismantling the mechanisms of accountability, destroying civil discourse, demeaning allies, debasing norms, despoiling institutional resources, dismissing government guardrails, and degrading the public trust in democratic institutions. Subsequent presidents will have to spend much of their bandwidth simply undoing the damage done.

But out of this devastation comes... what? Maybe Greensburg should be a model.

There's a wind farm about five miles southwest of town—ten wind turbines generating enough clean, renewable energy to power every home, business, and municipal building. One civic re-planner once explained, "It makes complete sense in Greensburg, where wind destroyed the town, to have wind help rebuild it."

Maybe the inevitable response to a cyclone of destruction in America is a movement of equal force. Imagine the United States as a small town in the middle of a desolate Kansas prairie. Maybe the welcome sign along the highway says "Land of the Free, Home of the Brave" or "Give Me Your Tired, Your Poor, Your Huddled Masses." Let's pretend there's a little Statue of Liberty there, too. In fact, there are more than two-dozen standing throughout Kansas. It's true. In 1950, the Boy Scouts of America placed some 200 replicas of Lady Liberty around the country. A hefty portion populate the Plains—in front of the high school in Coffeyville, the public library in Hays, the civic center in Independence, the county courthouse in Troy, the state capitol in Topeka.

Now imagine that devastating winds comes through town, perhaps in the form of a blowhard. The welcome signs disintegrate. The statue topples. The community that has survived so much for so long suddenly seems to be teetering on the brink of extinction, its spirit profoundly transformed, if not broken. So we ask what the folks in Greensburg wondered: What do we do next?

In July 2019, even before the president so mishandled a pandemic that the world began to pity what Ronald Reagan once described as the "shining city on a hill," a wonderful writer named Michelle Ruiz wrote a piece for Vogue.com in which she countered a plea from Thomas Friedman. After imploring Democrats to "just nominate a decent, sane person, one committed to reunifying the country and creating more good jobs," Friedman added, "But please, spare me the revolution! It can wait."

Ruiz didn't think so. She wrote that "lukewarmth" didn't seem the proper response to Muslim bans and immigrant children in cages and threats to reproductive rights and tax policies that further exacerbated income disparity. "It's a philosophy that simply doesn't match the urgency and passion of the moment," she explained. And then, pointing to the massive Women's March and the March for Our Lives and the "pink wave" of the midterm elections and the lawyers and doctors fighting against Muslim bans and dissolution of migrant families, she added, "It also ignores a powerful truth right in front of us: It's too late to spare anyone the revolution because the revolution is already happening."

A couple of months later, a political theorist named Serbulent Turan published an op-ed with this title: IS THE UNITED

STATES ON THE BRINK OF A REVOLUTION? It was a more academic take on the notion. "It seems to me the U.S. is currently showing all the signs political scientists and historians would identify in retrospect as conducive to a revolutionary uprising," he wrote, specifically citing tremendous economic inequality, a deep conviction that the ruling classes only serve themselves, and the rise of "political alternatives that were barely acceptable in the margins of society before." Turan also noted, eight months before George Floyd's death, that most major revolutions are preceded by an increase in protest, marches, petitions. And when the protesters' concerns are ignored, the aforementioned become more violent. This was before a president decided to tear gas peaceful protesters for a Bible-wielding photo-op.

I'm not saying we should start breaking out the guillotines. I doubt it would work, anyway, on a president who sticks his neck out for no one. But you know who does compare this moment to the French Revolution? An expert on the French Revolution. Rebecca Spang, professor of history at Indiana University, wrote a piece for *The Atlantic* during the early weeks of COVID lockdowns and protests: "Fear sweeps the land. Many businesses collapse. Some huge fortunes are made. Panicked consumers stockpile paper, food, and weapons. The government's reaction is inconsistent and ineffectual. Ordinary commerce grinds to a halt; investors can find no safe assets. Political factionalism grows more intense. Everything falls apart." She was describing France in 1789. "In hindsight a revolution may look like a single event, but they are never experienced that way. Instead they are extended periods in which the routines of normal life are dislocated and existing rituals lose their meaning," she wrote. "The

United States may not be having a revolution right now, but we are surely living in revolutionary times."

Of course, the bigger question is not whether we are in the midst of a profound transformation, but rather: Do we want to be?

When the most powerful man in the nation is attempting to sabotage free and fair elections and calling for the U.S. Justice Department to prosecute his political enemies, when voter suppression has become a mainstream political tactic, when the 50 richest Americans are worth as much as the poorest 165 million, when race has become so entrenched as a trigger point that one group can shout that they matter while another group takes offense at it, when 80 percent of the population thinks that the country is headed in the wrong direction, when American policy has been steered away from American goodness, it seems to me that upheaval is the answer—or even inevitable.

It may be time to not just redirect a nation, but repurpose it. Craft a system that caters to our general consciousness, rather than one that always lags behind. Don't just reform it; transform it through deep structural change. Every half-century or so, our country emerges stronger from what seemed at the time like cataclysmic turmoil—1787, 1865, 1920, 1968. Why not now? Break us, then remake us.

There is a storm coming. The wind is picking up. I've returned to Covfefe, and I'm staring through the windshield toward a bruising sky. Folks in Greensburg—everywhere in Kansas, actually—are well aware that the weather can change on a dime. I check my weather app, and my jaw drops. A strong early-season cold front is approaching. Temperatures are going to drop by as much as 60 degrees overnight. Gusts as high as 50 mph will drop the wind chill below freezing, from near record highs to record lows. Heavy rain is expected and, in parts of the High Plains, even early September snow.

And here I am sitting in a tin house on wheels on the open prairie. Just steps away, a concrete building smaller than Covfefe says SHELTER. Just the place where I'd want to cohabitate when a deadly respiratory virus is moving across the country as fast as the weather. But it'll do.

Anyway, the point is this: If a tempest is on its way, I'm ready.

SHOWDOWN

DODGE CITY, KANSAS

The Wickedest Little City in America. Queen of Cowtowns. Bibulous Babylon of the Frontier. Whatever it calls itself, Dodge City is a bit like your old-as-the-hills grandfather telling you tales about the mischief he used to make when he was your age. And Gramps has been coasting on that story for decades.

Sure, this was a wild and woolly Kansas trail town. You can still see the old wagon ruts from the Santa Fe Trail a few miles outside of the city, and over the course of a decade some five million cattle were driven here from Texas via the Western and Chisholm trails. And yes, there were enough shootouts in Wyatt Earp's jurisdiction—or at least tales of such—that one New York newspaper gushed, "There is more concentrated hell in Dodge City than any other place of equal size."

But I'm hunkered down for a couple days in the self-proclaimed Cowboy Capital of the World, waiting for the ill winds to blow past, and the sepia-toned throwback that the city is aiming for just feels cold and gray. Of course, that might be because it's very cold and gray. (Note: The good folks in Dodge City should remember to tell the people who aren't from Dodge City that the tornado siren is tested every Wednesday at noon. That was unpleasant.)

Dodge City remains a major cattle-shipping hub and a trade center for the regional wheat-growing industry. But the whole place feels like a hodgepodge of incongruities—sort of the way the Gunfighters' Wax Museum on 5th Avenue is located inside the Kansas Teachers Hall of Fame. There's a replica of Front Street, for instance, modeled after Front Street in 1876. It is very much... well, an approximation of what was. The whole city surely is.

Back in the day, folks like Earp and Bat Masterson kept an eye out for trouble at the Long Branch Saloon. The 1,200 residents—cattlemen, card sharks, buffalo hunters, railroad workers, soldiers, settlers—could choose from 19 businesses licensed to sell liquor. Nowadays, a few blocks from the replica Front Street, you can opt for a smoothie instead at the Snow Station Ice Cream Shop. Next door to the old saloon is a replica of G.M. Hoover Cigars, owned by the first elected mayor of Dodge City. These days, you can stop instead at Yogi's Vape, across from that ice cream shop. I don't spot a soul in the Tonsorial Parlor on old Front Street (back when dentists like Doc Holliday often doubled as barbers). But as I dodge the raindrops in Dodge City, I peek through a window to see that Demi's Brow and Beauty is packed with customers, their faces inches apart, not a protective face covering in sight.

Which brings me to perhaps the most depressing divide in America in 2020: The most basic of precautions, which reduces COVID transmission rates and which could serve as a unifying symbol of a nation standing together by standing apart, has somehow been politicized.

At the entrance to Dodge City's Boot Hill Museum is a printed sign: "Howdy partner! Thanks for wearing your face mask!" The image shown doesn't look like a fellow protecting himself and others from a deadly virus; he looks like he's about to rob a stagecoach. In fact, in Dodge City's wicked heyday, the bandanna was a utilitarian article of clothing. It could sling a broken arm, filter drinking water or coffee, serve as a wash rag, ward off the cold or the sun or the dust on a cattle drive. And of course, once in a while it was a useful tool for hiding an identity. Over the years, Hollywood turned it into a ubiquitous outlaw accoutrement. Bad guys wear masks. Somehow, this notion has filtered into the subconscious of an astoundingly self-interested segment of the population—they've replaced the greater good with the bad and the ugly.

This isn't new ground in a nation that doesn't learn from its missteps. In 1918, when the Spanish flu was devastating San Francisco, maskless marauders were charged with disturbing the peace. In response, an Anti-Mask League, claiming a violation of individual rights, managed to get the city ordinance repealed. But the flu-ravage continued—viruses tend to do that—and the law was reinstated.

Polls show a significant divide between Republicans and Democrats regarding mask mandates. Academics have pointed out that this emblem neatly fits into ideological perspectives that cleave a nation in two. On the Right, core beliefs about personal freedom, government overreach, a distrust of science, and fears of collective actions that hint at—gasp!—socialism. Not to mention relentless loyalty to a president who may rank as the most disloyal human being on the planet. On the Left, faith in the role of government, the balance between liberty and security, the need to contribute to the public good.

But let's boil it down to its simplest form. Wearing a mask can save lives. Not wearing a mask puts more lives at risk. Toss out the grand ideological reference points, and call anti-masking what it is: a symbol of distorted notions of freedom, of performative masculinity, of cowardice misjudged as manliness, of all-about-me-ism, of not-my-problem-ism. It was a call to action on the part of medical experts, but a swath of America has decided to decline the call and purposefully do the wrong thing. As Wyatt Earp once said, "Are you gonna do somethin'? Or are you just gonna stand there and bleed?"

So I prefer some stronger language on the wear-a-mask signs, like this one that skated around Twitter: "Mask Required For Service. Do not pout. Do not whine. Do not argue. Do not harass the employees. Do not spout conspiracy theories or regurgitate information you got from your dumb uncle on Facebook. This isn't political; it is basic health and safety. Do not choose to be the reason the rest of the world is laughing at us. 'I forgot it in my car.' Well, go get it then. 'This is unconstitutional.' No, it's not. 'This is a hoax.' You're an idiot."

Frankly, when it comes to a public health crisis, I feel shaming has its place. The irony of the conflict is that a face covering has long conveyed a kind of toughness—for Wild West anti-heroes, for costumed superheroes, for miners warding off black lung disease. But during this pandemic, going barefaced has been become, in the eyes of far too many people, a warped display of machismo. And it seems to be as peculiarly American as High Noon and high COVID death rates.

The biggest outlaw, of course, is the president of the grab-them-by-the-posse. Trump tried wearing a mask for a while. He tweeted that he felt like the Lone Ranger. The Twitterverse promptly replied, "The Lone Ranger's mask had two eyeholes in it. Trump's just has one asshole in it." Of course, his flirtation with actual role-modeling was short lived. Instead, he began to say about Joe Biden, "Did you ever see a man that likes a mask so much?" While the U.S. continued to lead the world in COVID cases, he added, "It gives him a feeling of security. If I was a psychiatrist, I'd say this guy has some big issues."

Projection (noun): The attribution of one's own ideas, feelings, or attitudes to other people or to objects (especially the externalization of blame, guilt, or responsibility as a defense against anxiety).

What makes it all the more astounding is the fact that Trump is famously germaphobic. Back in the summer of 2019, before the pandemic made all reasonable thinkers take precautions, Politico ran a whole article titled THE PURELL PRESIDENCY, describing him as "the most germ-conscious man to ever lead the free world." Remember, this was roughly seven months before Trump heard about the true dangers of COVID-19 and decided not to fully disclose it to the public.

The story discussed how his personal aide carries a bottle of hand sanitizer at all times and how under-the-weather staffers know to steer clear of a man who would be "extremely annoyed by that," a notion validated by a moment during an interview with ABC's George Stephanopoulos. Acting chief of staff Mick Mulvaney started coughing, and Trump paused the interview, shook his head, and said, "I don't like that. If you're going to cough, please, leave the room." How dare someone in the Oval Office risk other peoples' health.

A generation ago, during a 1993 interview with Howard Stern, Trump admitted that his germ-aversion—the fact that he washes his hands "as many times as possible" during the day—"could be a psychological problem." Regarding washing before eating, the 2019 Politico piece even offered that Trump "religiously follows protocols from the Centers for Disease Control and Prevention."

But apparently, not during a deadly pandemic.

Trump has long shunned handshakes (unless, of course, he can turn it into a virtual arm-wrestling match in a pathetic display of alpha-male-wannabeism). Over the years, he has called the practice "barbaric" and "disgusting." In his 1997 book *The Art of the Comeback*, he wrote, "One of the curses of American society is the simple act of shaking hands, and the more successful and famous one becomes the worse this terrible custom seems to get." In fact, it's one reason why people around him were so surprised that he would actually run for president. Rope lines? Kissing babies? Pressing the flesh in a New Hampshire coffee shop? He was asked about it in 1999, when he first put his presidential ambitions on display. "Maybe we'll change something there," Trump said. Then he added, "They have medical reports all the time. Shaking hands, you catch colds, you catch the flu, you catch it, you catch all sorts of things." Even during the Ebola outbreak of 2014, Trump tweeted, "Something very important, and indeed society changing, may come out of the Ebola epidemic that will be a very good thing: NO SHAKING HANDS!"

But then came the coronavirus, and a choice—safety or showmanship. Model the experts' suggested behaviors? Or do the exact opposite in an effort to project masculinity and insusceptibility, shrug off the virus's severity, and mitigate your own culpability? It seemed, particularly to observers who have long known of his bacillophobia, that Trump began to *deliberately* shake hands—at a televised town hall in Scranton, at a rally in Charleston, at Mar-a-Lago, in the Oval Office. When a reporter questioned him about it because, you know, that's how pandemics get worse, Trump—world-class germaphobe and handshake denier—answered, "Because it almost becomes a habit."

About a week later, on the day he declared a national emergency, Trump said, "I want to encourage everyone to follow the guidelines we have issued by CDC and these common-sense measures. A lot of it is common sense." That was amid a Rose Garden display with various CEOs and health officials that turned into a parade of handshakes. These supposed saviors were all but licking the microphone, one by one—until one CEO offered Trump an elbow bump instead. "Practice that," he suggested.

"That's good," said Trump. "I like that." But he didn't.

This is what someone wrote about Dodge City in 1877: "Some things occur in Dodge that the world never knows of. Probably it is best so. Other things occur that leak out by degrees, notwithstanding the use of hush money. That, too, is perhaps the best. Men learn by such means." Doesn't that sound like President Despicable? Only he doesn't learn.

In the *Wyatt Earp* movie, there is a scene in which Doc Holliday is introduced to a Dodge City lawman whom he despises. "Forgive me," Holliday says, "if I don't shake hands." He suffered from tuberculosis. It is thought to be the reason he headed west, hoping for a more suitable climate. But his famous reply was predicated more on defiance than defense of health. Trump, remarkably, started actually shaking hands for the same reason.

And, of course, he deliberately does NOT wear a mask. By not covering his face, he's trying to cover his ass.

During my cross-country trek, he and his top aides have appeared maskless at myriad events, again disregarding guidelines from his own task force and the CDC. Twice during the Republican National Convention, Trump attended large events without wearing a mask. In a fit of Darwinian monkey-see-monkey-don't, almost no one in the crowd did either. He has met with top officials from New Hampshire to North Carolina without a face covering. Biden's response: "Presidents are supposed to lead, not engage in folly and be falsely masculine."

But Trump is Superman, remember? He couldn't possibly contract the virus, right? It would expose him as reckless. It would undermine his all-too-frequent contentions that we've been controlling a pandemic. It would force him, theoretically at least, into unfamiliar territories—transparency, vulnerability, humility. It wouldn't possibly lead him to veer further in the wrong direction, right?

The damage is done. Trump's refusal to regularly cover his face has cemented it as a partisan issue that feeds the tinfoil hat-wearing crowd—the conspiracy theorists (China-made masks!), the COVID-hoaxsters, the anti-vaxxers, the masks-make-you-sicker morons. There is truth in this generalization: If there's a MAGA hat, you're unlikely to find a mask. So it is no surprise that the Great Plains lags behind other regions in the percentage of regular mask wearers. Kansas is among the most intransigent states. Early in the summer, Democratic Governor Laura Kelly mandated a statewide mask order. But officials in 90 of the state's 105 counties opted out of the law that allowed local leaders to do as they wish in response. That included Ford County where Dodge City is a center of the meatpacking industry, leading to the highest rate of cases in the state.

Governor Kelly tried to appeal to reason. "This is not about state and local control, and it's not a question of personal freedom," she said. "This is a matter of social responsibility while we're dealing with the worst outbreak of a communicable virus in a century." Yet one weekly Kansas newspaper published by a county Republican Party chairman posted a cartoon depicting Kelly wearing a mask with a Jewish Star of David on it, next to a drawing of people being loaded onto train cars. The caption: "Lockdown Laura says: Put on your mask ... and step onto the cattle car."

All through the summer, mouth-breathers have been making anti-mask stands, sometimes violent ones, like a town drunk waltzing into a saloon and waving a pistol. It's not enough that essential workers have to trudge to work in a pandemic. Now they have to practice conflict resolution because Costco and Trader Joe's have become battlefields in a culture war. In Flint, Michigan, a store security guard was murdered for refusing a mask-less patron entry into a Family Dollar store. In San Antonio, a passenger attacked a bus driver who asked him to wear a mask. In Phoenix, an American Airlines passenger hit a gate agent who told her she couldn't board without a mask. In Baton Rouge, three women were arrested after attacking a Chili's hostess—a 17-year-old girl—for enforcing social distancing. In Austin, a drunk 25-year-old pushed a park ranger into a lake for doing the same. And in North Carolina, a group called Reopen N.C. plopped a mask (or "submission muzzle," as they called it) into a pan, set it on fire, and cooked a hot dog over the open flames.

They say adversity introduces us to ourselves. We have stepped through the looking glass in America, and the rest of the world truly cannot believe it.

Anti-lockdown protests are the stupid cousin to anti-mask demonstrations. In Topeka last spring, scores of participants were smothered in stars and stripes, as if suggesting that honest attempts to protect Americans are somehow anti-American. They painted their cars and posters. LIVE FREE OR DIE... MAKE KANSAS OPEN AGAIN... WHICH RIGHT IS NEXT? One protester in a "Trump 2020" T-shirt held a pair of signs—one ideologically convoluted (SOCIALIST GOV. KELLY IS A DICTATOR THAT RULES LIKE PUTIN) and the other irrationally hyperbolic (GOV. KELLY'S POWER GRAB WILL KILL MORE THAN THE VIRUS CAN KILL). That was in April, when 50,000 Americans had died. As I write this, we're passing 200,000.

One of the most famous graveyards of the Old West was Boot Hill Cemetery, the site of the modern-day museum and Front Street replica in Dodge City. The story goes that a cowboy was killed in a gunfight in 1872. He was a drifter, friendless, anonymous, so he was wrapped in a blanket and buried with his boots on, right where he fell. For the next six years, anyone who died with enough money or community standing was buried in the cemetery at nearby Fort Dodge. The rest were dumped in Boot Hill: Jack Reynolds, shot six times by a track layer. Charles "Texas" Hill and Ed Williams, killed in a dance hall by the city's "Vigilance Committee." Jack Wagner, died during a shootout with Ed Masterson. George Hoy, shot by Wyatt Earp.

It is a bygone reminder of bad choices.

There's a newspaper photograph that I can't seem to erase from my psyche—not of a 19th-century gunslinger, but rather a 21st-century version. He's a burly, bearded fellow from Dodge City who attended the Topeka protest. The photo shows him with a huge U.S. flag in one hand, a semi-automatic rifle in the other, and a tattoo on his right arm: IF YOU WANT PEACE, PREPARE FOR WAR. All in the service of protesting an effort to keep people safe during a global pandemic.

And I'm thinking, *Really? Is that the hill you want to die on?*

NO PLACE LIKE HOME

LIBERAL, KANSAS

The rains have come and gone, leaving a quiet emptiness as I slice southwest down U.S. 54 toward the seat of Seward County, butting up against the Oklahoma Panhandle. "There's no place like Liberal, Kansas!" shouts the billboard leading into town. But actually, there seem to be lots of places like it—flatland outposts with economies revolving around farming, trucking, ethanol production, and especially the beef industry. Some 3,500 residents, nearly one-fifth of the city's population, work for National Beef Packing. Just south of here are feedlots rather shocking in their massiveness—cattle penned from the highway to the horizon.

I wouldn't describe Liberal as charming—functional, maybe. In 1541, Francisco Vasquez de Coronado marched north from the Rio Grande, seeking the fabled kingdom of gold. When he found instead only this gray prairie, he had his guide executed. Not that Liberal doesn't try hard to entice passersby. Again, I'm zapped with a memory from *National Lampoon's Vacation*, when Clark Griswold considers "shooting over to 54 and zipping down to Liberal."

"What for?"

"The House of Mud."

"What's the House of Mud?"

"It's only the largest freestanding mud dwelling ever built, that's all."

There is no House of Mud in Liberal. However... Visit the Mid-America Air Museum, the fifth largest collection of civilian and military aircraft in the nation! Watch women sprint through the streets while flipping pancakes on International Pancake Day! Come see the Land of Oz! The latter, tucked behind a gas station, welcomes you with amateurish cardboard cutouts, a dusty Yellow Brick Road, and an earnest local actress, who narrates Dorothy's adventures featuring special and not-so-special effects.

Liberal wasn't named for its politics, but for its generosity. In 1885, a homesteader named S.S. Rogers filed a claim for 160 acres here, opened a general store, and dug a deep well. Water was scarce and often sold for high prices, but Rogers offered it to travelers without charge. "That's mighty liberal of ya," they would respond. Soon, Rogers became known as "that liberal fella." When the postmistress (who would become his wife) opened the first post office inside the general store, the town became known as Liberal. I find the story to be somewhat dubious, but I sure do appreciate the red state reminder that liberal means magnanimous, abundant, openhanded. Of course, naming things isn't Liberal's strong suit. Its semi-pro baseball team, winner of several national titles and honoring American League founder Ban Johnson, is the Liberal Bee Jays. And its high school nickname was a topic of public discussion at a school board meeting a few weeks before my arrival, though I still can't fathom how there can be any debate about in 2020. They're still called the Redskins.

Yeah, Liberal looks pretty typical to me. And it is. But it certainly isn't. Perhaps I should clarify, which requires a dive into changing demographics, perhaps the most salient driver of the Us vs. Them disaster that has befallen this nation.

Demographics are the greatest threat to the long-term survival of the Republican Party. It's not just that young voters lean Democratic, setting up a foundational shift that could last decades. In fact, the entire under-18 U.S. population is now majority non-white. In less than a decade, the under-30 population will be, too. And it's not just that women are running screaming from a party with a misogynistic figurehead who cheated on his pregnant wife with a porn star, but hopes to overturn Roe v. Wade. It's simply the obvious fact that the current version of the GOP is indistinguishable from Trumpism, and the demographics to which that appeals are shrinking in influence. Meanwhile, the groups most maligned and antagonized by the politics of division are exploding.

In 2016, white citizens represented nearly 62 percent of the U.S. population and 71 percent of all voters, thus exerting a disproportionate impact on the outcome of the election. But America is growing more diverse—quickly and inexorably. By 2044, the U.S. is expected to have become majority-minority—no race or ethnicity will represent a majority of the population. By 2060, non-white Americans are estimated to constitute 56 percent of the populace.

Politically, the enormous shift calls for big-tent politics, particularly because America's swing states are showing the most significant demographic change. In fact, two electoral giants—Florida and Texas—are witnessing the fastest minority population growth. After Barack Obama was elected president in 2012, the GOP's postmortem suggested a need for recalibration. Reach out to minorities and women. Soften language. Become more inclusive. But with Trump at the helm, the party has careened in the other direction. Of course, he's just the latest iteration of an appeal to racial bias that began a half-century ago with Richard Nixon's "Southern strategy." But Trump's short-term calculations and scapegoating rhetoric have only made a bad situation much worse. Most every megatrend says the Republicans are, as Harvard professor Thomas Patterson put it, "sitting on a demographic time bomb of their own making."

Patterson has pointed out that a generation ago roughly two-thirds of Asian-Americans—a large portion of them small business owners with high family incomes—voted Republican. Today, they vote Democratic by the same margin. And what does Trump do? He panders to prejudice during a pandemic, calling it the "Chinese Virus" when he knows full well that this feeds bigotry from his acolytes toward the fastest-growing ethnic group in America. Likewise, the Latino community—a diverse demographic itself, including many who are deeply religious and pro-life—might have been ripe for Republican embrace. But Trump's strategy? Build a physical and metaphorical wall. Demonize immigrants. Turn away refugees. Kidnap children at the border. Lose track of their parents. The Latino share of the population has grown in every state since 2000, and according to a 2019 poll, most believe the GOP is actively "hostile" toward them. And, of course, as Trump has disingenuously embraced evangelicals, he has correspondingly alienated the LGBTQ community.

Of course, race doesn't always correlate exactly with voting patterns. Vermont, for instance, is the second whitest state in the country—and arguably the most liberal. But Patterson did an analysis, based solely on population change estimates, of the GOP's projected future. His conclusion: Should current voting patterns hold, by 2032 Democrats would receive 59 percent of the vote. That's seismic.

Psychologists have studied this phenomenon of demographic movement. A sense of race identity can be somewhat dormant among those in the majority, but it suddenly becomes prominent when there is a perceived "threat" to that position—as if it is a zero-sum scenario in which the rise of one group implies the demise of their own. Just like the threat of death makes people more conservative, so does the threat of losing the comfort of the majority.

Hence, the ugliness: The dog-whistle rhetoric about "protecting our heritage" and "saving your neighborhoods." The fear-mongering about rapist immigrants and invading caravans and terrorist refugees. Manipulation of racial resentment—white anxiety about a changing world—is the fulcrum of Trumpism. Cynical politicians have been stoking those fears, implicitly and explicitly. But, even more shamelessly, they've also manipulated the system in an attempt to disenfranchise Democratic-leaning demographic groups.

It is no accident that America sent a white nationalist to the White House in the very first presidential election after the Supreme Court gutted the Voting Rights Act.

Republican-controlled states were able to redraw legislative maps, gerrymandering districts into unrecognizability in a largely successful effort to create favorable outcomes. The Fourth Court of Appeals struck down much of North Carolina's attempt, claiming that it targeted African Americans "with almost surgical precision" and imposed cures "for problems that did not exist." When that wasn't enough, state legislators pushed through harsh voting restrictions, making it more difficult for left-leaning constituencies to cast ballots. The North Carolina Republican Party actually sent out a press release boasting about how it drove down Black voter turnout.

In 2020, the efforts have become even more obvious and extreme. The blueprint might be compared to the Trump Administration's COVID-19 response, but instead of incompetence, this is a strategy map for insidiousness. The tactics fall under two broad categories.

1. **Game the system.** Welcome deception when it suits you. Shout "rigged election" when it doesn't. Do almost nothing to thwart—or even acknowledge—brazen foreign interference in the U.S. election because it's what got you elected last time around. But spew rumors of widespread voter fraud—a nearly nonexistent issue. Convene a White House commission to prove that you wouldn't have lost the popular vote handily if only millions of people hadn't voted illegally. Vow to end this scourge on democracy. And then shrug when the commission is shut down after 11 months, having found a grand total of... nothing. So change tactics. Sow seeds of doubt about the safety and viability of mail-in ballots, just to raise confusion

on Election Day. Then game the system so that votes aren't counted. Appoint a major Republican donor as Postmaster General, and then sabotage the U.S. Postal Service so that it's more difficult to deliver those ballots—which Democrats are most likely to cast—on time. Cut post office hours. Reduce overtime. Force half-filled trucks to set out on their rounds. And then complain about what a mess mail-in voting will be.

2.   **Suppress the vote.** In a nation with shamefully low voter turnout, make voting harder, not easier. Block online voter registration, as nine GOP-led states have. Purge voter rolls. Enact strict voter ID laws that disproportionately affect minorities. Allow a gun permit to serve as a voter ID, but not a student ID card. Disenfranchise people who have already served time for felony convictions. Fight hard for in-person voting during a deadly pandemic. Sue states to prevent them from allowing voting by mail. Block mail-in ballots and force would-be voters to re-request them. Require a witness to sign mail ballots—two if you're in Alabama. When that doesn't do the job and enthusiastic voters are still determined to cast a ballot, simply make it physically harder to do so. Close hundreds and hundreds of polling places so that Americans—well into the 21st century—have to stand in line for hours just to cast a damn vote. Recruit poll watchers, including perhaps the neo-Nazi Proud Boys. Tell them to "stand by." Threaten, as Trump also has done, to send law enforcement to watch the polls, which is illegal. If voters want to drop off mail

ballots in person, turn it into a trek. Ohio's Republican secretary of state defied a court order and imposed a limit of one drop box per county. Texas's GOP governor even ordered counties to remove drop boxes, forcing a single drop-off location for Harris County's 2.5 million eligible voters. Conversely but equally perversely, California's GOP threw subtlety to the wind and actually installed unofficial drop-off boxes.

All of this infuriates me, not as a liberal but as an American. And it all comes down to the Republican Party fearing—and spreading fear about—changing demographics, which begins to seep into the psyche of the average American. So even as the nation becomes more diverse, much of the white population chooses to flee the diversity, thus missing out on the face-to-face interactions that generally assuage fears and enlighten—about the contribution of immigrants, the feasibility of assimilation, the benefits of diversity.

To see such success, who would think you would have to travel to Liberal, Kansas?

I pull into a random parking lot near the center of town, between La Casa del Pastor Mexican Restaurant and Carniceria, a grocery store that also houses La Canasta meat market. It's near El Tule Auto Sales, not far from Mi Tierra, Super Pollo, Fruteria Ojinaga, Las 3 Marias, and Gordita 2 Go. I'm steps away from a taco truck—El Pastorcito. Cars are pulling in and out of the lot. Some customers are there for the food truck. Others, a couple of them in American flag face coverings, rush in and out of Carniceria.

Kansas as a whole is roughly 86 percent white. But something remarkable has happened in Liberal—in fact, to a significant portion of the state. Over the past couple of decades, thousands of Latino immigrants have been settling in southwest Kansas, most of them hoping to secure better-than-minimum-wage meatpacking jobs in the "beef triangle" around Dodge City, Garden City, and Liberal. The tri-county area, where segregation once reigned, is now majority-minority.

While Liberal's population has declined over the past decade, the Latino portion of it has skyrocketed to nearly 62 percent—about five times higher than the state average. One white woman who has lived in Liberal for more than half a century told a local reporter that while she had to learn to accept diversity, it came naturally to her children and grandchildren. "Our young people know how to interact with people from other cultures," she said. "That's really a positive thing."

This city has been transformed into a bit of a multicultural model. Liberal hosts a rodeo every August and celebrates Ozfest in October, but the Cinco de Mayo Fiesta is the centerpiece of spring—in fact, one of the largest cultural events in southwest Kansas. Liberal also annually hosts an African American Celebration and a Cultural Diversity Day. Here's what the local chamber of commerce says about the latter: "Many immigrants from Asia, Mexico, and other parts of Latin America have relocated to Liberal in the past decade to fulfill their dreams. To celebrate this great diversity, people representing more than 40 nationalities gather annually in Liberal to eat, dance, and discover the uniqueness of each ethnic group."

It's not all cupcakes and rainbows. There is a high transient population that moves between the three cities, Latino gangs have sprouted up in the area, and political representation lags far behind. There is only one Latino elected official among the 28 men and women on the commissions that run Ford, Finney, and Seward counties. But an increasing number of Latino businesses are making an economic and cultural impact on life in the region. More than that, as demographics change, the way folks in Liberal speak has even transformed. A Kansas State University researcher found that the city's young residents, even if they don't speak Spanish, have developed their own "Liberal accent." It's sort of a linguistic hybrid that mimics Spanish speech patterns—more staccato syllables, less nasal vowel pronunciations, an infusion of Spanish slang. Much the same thing has been happening in other U.S. regions with growing Latino populations. So Liberal—a self-proclaimed "Crossroads of Commerce"—is actually an intersection of so much more.

As I'm scanning the taco truck's menu, a worker with a sweet smile—I later find out her name is Maricela—approaches me. She roams the parking lot like an old-fashioned carhop, taking your order and delivering your food. Maricela has two vital suggestions: Try the taco lengua. And talk to the man—she points—right there, the diminutive, busy-looking fellow gliding by in his truck. That's how I meet Adolfo.

Adolfo Almaraz was born in Zacatecas in central Mexico nearly a half-century ago, the fourth of 15 children, the youngest of whom died at birth. The family moved to Guadalajara when he was six. Starting in elementary school, he worked a series of jobs—bricklayer, plumber, electrician, taquero, butcher. He never finished high school. He wanted to work. And at 17, he decided he wanted to work in America.

We're standing inside La Casa del Pastor, trying to have a conversation through face coverings and language challenges and the sound of workers refashioning the whole place for a "grand reopening" once the pandemic has passed. A painted sign on the wall says, "The Three Pilars of our Business: 1. Our Employees 2. Our Employees 3. Our Employees." The misspelling of "Pilars" is understandable because the same painted sign next to it—in Spanish—says "Los Pilares."

"Who'd you come over with?" I ask Adolfo.

"I was by myself."

He crossed the border on a rainy day and soon made it to Los Angeles, where he looked up an address he had been given, only to discover that a relative of his no longer lived there. For a while Adolfo slept on the streets, until an acquaintance let him sleep in a truck parked in front of his house. Adolfo's journey eventually took him wherever there were rumors of opportunity. "Just looking for a good place to grow my family," he says. He drove to Utah, Las Vegas, finally Denver, where he opened a meat shop to middling success.

Adolfo proudly shows me a mural he commissioned, painted on a wall in La Casa del Pastor. It depicts many representations of Kansas—a locomotive, a sturdy steer, a wheat-bearing wagon, sunflowers in full bloom. The main focus is an ethnically diverse collection of people frolicking in a waterfall of sorts, only the waters overflow from two massive cupped hands above them. I suppose it signifies that a higher power has provided bounty and opportunity.

Dorothy Gale is there, too, standing along a Yellow Brick Road, distanced from a twister painted in the corner of the mural. I'm wondering if Adolfo even realizes the analogies to his life—the whirlwind of transplanting from the only world you've known to one entirely unfamiliar, the wonder of opening a door to possibilities and then finding a path toward deliverance, and the myriad obstacles along the way. The Wicked Witch of widespread xenophobia. A Cowardly Lion in the White House, scapegoating the disenfranchised in an effort to spread fear and prop up his precarious manhood. A Haunted Forest of language and cultural barriers: "I'D TURN BACK IF I WERE YOU." The shameful narrative that, like sleep-inducing poppies, reimagines a nation of immigrants as a collection of entrenched Americans dead set on protecting a shared heritage. And the very real prospect that the American Dream might be revealed, Wizard-like, as only a sham of smoke and mirrors.

Right about the time he became an American citizen, Adolfo took a wrong turn on a highway. He had been aiming for Olathe, Kansas, but wound up in Dodge City. So he stayed there. Adolfo was working as consistently as he could, saving as much as he dared, chasing an elusive dream, and by now he was married with children. He and his wife had saved money for a vacation. In Dodge City, they decided to spend it instead on a potential future. "A concessions trailer," Adolfo tells me. A taco truck. El Pastorcito.

Dodge City was a challenge. The city required him to register his business as temporary, meaning he had to obtain costly temporary business permits. He also was required to move to a different location every three months, but most property owners wanted to rent annually. When it was time to get out of Dodge, Adolfo heard about a building available in Liberal, 80 miles away. Various businesses had tried and failed at the location. Adolfo figured he had nothing to lose. Well, except everything.

"I love Liberal," says Adolfo of a place some 1,300 miles north of his native world. "They let me grow the business."

At first, he rented space in the parking lot, setting up his trailer for business. Then he bought the building. Then he formed a company, Carniceria La Canasta LLC, and expanded. Now he owns the Mexican restaurant on one side of the lot, the grocery store on the other, the food truck, and a couple more buildings down to the corner. He has an office down the street. He's training employees, hiring contractors, consulting with human resources experts. He has plans. Big plans.

"Well, I have a lot of dreams. I have a... " He struggles to find the proper word in English. "I have a purpose—my dream."

"And what's that?"

He pauses. I can tell by his eyes that he's smiling. "Live a legend."

Amid this largely dispiriting journey, I think those three words might constitute my favorite moment.

ARBITRARY AMERICA

TEXHOMA, OKLAHOMA / TEXHOMA, TEXAS

F unny how you can be rolling along a straight stretch of highway—some 200 miles along U.S. 54 from Liberal in Kansas
toward Tucumcari in New Mexico—and yet still take myriad
off ramps. The mind has a GPS of its own. As I pass by a great
grain elevator looming over the Panhandle town of Texhoma,
here in the heart of cattle country, the synapses send peripheral
thoughts my way...

Portmanteau. That's what you get when you merge the
sounds and meanings of two different words—for example, when
chuckle and snort are combined to make chortle. Texhoma
is a portmanteau. It's also a divided city—900 residents live
in Texhoma, Oklahoma, and just over 300 reside in Texhoma,
Texas. The former is in Cimmaron County, the latter in Sherman
County. Different zip codes and insurance rates and income
taxes, separate municipal governments, but a joint school district—an elementary school in Texas, a high school in Oklahoma.

Even the locals are a bit unsure of where one state ends and
the other begins. In the early 1930s a mistake was discovered in
the 1860 survey of the state line, and a resurvey moved the border
465 feet south of the original State Line Road, which meant that

most of the town's businesses moved from Texas to Oklahoma without moving an inch. In fact, Texas Road still runs parallel to the state line—but it's in Oklahoma.

Dozens of portmanteaus populate the fine print of the American atlas, many of them unincorporated blips or settlements that once were—Kensee (Kentucky and Tennessee), Idavada (Idaho-Nevada), Wyocolo (Wyoming-Colorado), Dakomin (South Dakota-Minnesota). Some states are portmanteau-prolific—there are six each in California and Arkansas. Some borders even double up. Along the Delaware-Maryland line, there's both a Delmar and a Marydel. Along Alabama and Florida, there's a Alaflora and a Florala. Along Arkansas and Missouri, we have Arkmo and Moark. Colorado-Kansas has both Cokan and Kanco. Along Texas-Louisiana, there's a Texla and—get this—a Latex. Oh, and along the border to Mexico, there's both a Calexico and a Mexicali.

To make it all the more convoluted, there are a half-dozen towns that combine three state names. One of them is unique in that it's three separate words—Cal Nev Ari. The other five are Kenova (Kentucky, Ohio, West Virginia), Kentenia (Kentucky, Tennessee, Virginia), Okeana (Ohio, Kentucky, Indiana), Penowa (Pennsylvania, Ohio, West Virginia), and Texarkana (Texas, Arkansas, Louisiana). The latter is about 30 miles from the Louisiana border.

Now my imagination runs to the towns that aren't—the possible variations. Connecticut and Rhode Island. No, Connect Island seems paradoxical. Iowa and Illinois. Eh, Ionois would be pronounced "I annoy." Washington and Oregon? Washgon sounds like a laundry detergent.

Fifty miles later, I stop for a while to rest in Dalhart, Texas, a center of agribusiness bookended by enormous cattle feedlots that look like a bovine version of a Trump super-spreader rally. Dalhart is a portmanteau straddling Dallam and Hartley counties, which takes me musing down an unplanned road about word combinations, which leads me to a mental side street about "sniglets."

Sniglets were a briefly popular lexicographic fad in the early '80s, introduced on the HBO comedy series *Not Necessarily the News*. They sit on that nostalgic shelf in my brain alongside Smurfs and Swatch Watches. A sniglet was any word that should be in the dictionary, but isn't—portmanteau-ish creations like "barcathrottle" (the gear shift on the side of a recliner) and "snackmosphere" (that pocket of air inside a potato chip bag). "Elecelleration" is the mistaken notion that the more you press the elevator button, the faster the elevator will arrive. If you possess the ability to turn the bathtub faucet with your toes, you're "aquadextrous." A person who always pushes on a door marked "pull." That's a "doork."

Memories of these absurdities start to pinball around my cranium, which provides a nice escape from the usual impending doom scenarios. I'm reminded of the oddities and excesses of the Eighties, and—naturally—that gets me thinking about the oddities and excesses of Donald Trump. There actually is a word called "trumpery." As a noun, the dictionary defines it as "an attractive article of little value or use." As an adjective: "showy but worthless." It's hard to improve on the real thing, but I try anyway, spending the next 40 miles conjuring up sniglets regarding the doork in the Oval Office:

DISPLOMACY: The act of treating enemies like allies and allies like enemies

GIBBERICH: Incredibly affluent, yet stunningly ineloquent

NOKAYING: Repeatedly using the traditional hand sign for "okay" when you're clearly saying something that isn't

INTERJEKYLLTIONS: Hyperbolic self-interruptions revealing that a speaker is obviously reading a speech for the first time

NEPOTIZZY: An angry response, lashing out at truth-tellers when a son or daughter is caught lying

NASTIFARIAN: A physically unattractive man so high on himself that he frequently insults women for their appearance

IGNORAMIFICATIONS: Potentially catastrophic outcomes as a result of widespread willful ignorance (see 2016 Election)

EPITHET-TIC: The inability to stop giving others nicknames that actually fit you better

LINGUISTWIST: The transcription of an interview that shows an inability to complete a proper sentence

NARCISS-SCHISM: A willingness to exacerbate a nation's divisions in an effort to satisfy a desire for power and attention

INSOLVENSEASICK: Nauseated while watching someone else misinterpret several bankruptcies as a sign of financial genius

NEO-NOT-SEE: The political choice to feign ignorance regarding the true agenda of the alt-right

GRASP-HOLE: A jerk who attempts to dominate by turning a handshake into a tug-of-war

PU-TIN-EARED: A tendency to disregard even the possibility of collusion despite a pattern of stealth, selective amnesia, and stunning falsehoods

FLYNN-FLAMMERY: Serving as national security advisor despite being a paid agent of a foreign government

DO-REY-COMEY: A false note, usually involving the firing of an FBI director

PSCYHOPHANT: A Republican congressman who enables a sociopathic president

G.O.PEEING: Pissing away your country just to strengthen your party

HILLAREFLUX: The act of constantly, even four years later, regurgitating words like "emails" and "Benghazi"

PASSBUCKISM: A cowardly philosophy regarding accepting responsibility

PRESI-DENTAL: Having a constant urge to lie through your teeth while leading the executive branch

DEFIBULATE: The process, perhaps decades long, of restoring a nation's faith in science and fact

TRUMP-PENCE: A worthless piece of currency

If the folks zooming past me on the other side of the highway could see my face as I cruise through the Texas Panhandle, they'd raise an eyebrow at my stupid grin.

Just before the tiny village of Nara Visa, I cross into New Mexico, my first blue state since I passed through a sliver of southern Illinois. Of course, southern Illinois is hardly blue. But that's the problem with the Electoral College system. It forces generalizations and categorizations that don't necessarily reflect reality. In the 2016 election, nearly 4.5 million Californians voted for Trump. Nearly 3.9 million Texans voted for Hillary Clinton. None of those votes counted. We call Alabama a hard-red state, but 35 percent of registered voters identify as Democrats.

Vermont is the land of Bernie and Ben & Jerry's, but close to one-third of its residents voted for Trump.

My reverie returns to its origins—Texhoma. A satellite view of the town suggests that the state line runs directly through several homes—indeed, local historians tell stories about how one house had a living room in Oklahoma and a bedroom in Texas. Political divisions might be just as strange. Should Texas actually go blue—and it will someday soon—there might be two neighbors living a few dozen feet apart who may be politically likeminded, perhaps even filling out their ballots together. But one lives in a red state, the other in a blue.

There are a great many arguments against the continued use of the Electoral College system—not the least being, of course, that there have been more presidents lately who lost the popular vote than won it. When a man can garner nearly three million fewer national votes, pull an inside straight because of geographical quirks, ascend to the most powerful position in the world, and then govern as if only the red states are his constituency, that's not a functioning republic. When all but three Supreme Court seats can be filled by presidents who received fewer votes than their opponents, that's a profound flaw that needs fixing.

The Electoral College also distorts presidential campaigns by vastly overemphasizing swing states—and then distorts policy by motivating candidates to cater to the impulses of those states. It allows third party candidates almost no opportunity to win a national election, but many ways to tip the scales. And, of course, this archaic winner-take-all system makes a mockery of the one-person, one-vote principal. In fact, because electoral votes are based on congressional representation—and because a place like Wyoming (barely half a million residents) and California (nearly 40 million) have the same number of U.S. senators—it allows the folks in Laramie to have far more voting power than the people in Los Angeles.

But somewhat lost amid the statistical arguments against it are the psychological effects. About a dozen years ago, a trio of psychologists published a study titled "Seeing Red (and Blue): Effects of Electoral College Depictions on Political Group Perception." Basically, they had participants view electoral maps. Some were stark red vs. blue; others offered shades of purple based on the proportion of votes in each state—thus a more accurate reflection of political attitudes. The researchers contended that, while there is certainly a political divide in America, red vs. blue maps "do more than passively describe the current state of affairs." In other words, they don't just reflect polarization; they exacerbate the situation. Even when numerical data was included, the simple colors of the map itself led participants to perceive the nation as more politically divided, stereotype the attitudes of each state's residents, and view people in each state's political minority as having less political agency. And, of course, the latter is true. Voter turnout is higher in swing states where citizens don't feel reduced by the system.

So red vs. blue has come to signify far more than political disagreements; it has become shorthand for core attitudes, cultural backgrounds, religious convictions. Merely the perception of that divide feeds bias, thwarts compromise, intensifies acrimony—implying a deeper divide, a more fundamental chasm. As the researchers put it, "Maps can do much more than describe: they can also persuade, obscure, and deceive."

It has reached the point where there are movements afoot to actually redraw the map in order to meet perceived cultural and political commonalities. An attempt called Greater Idaho, for instance, wants to force a ballot initiative that would let Idaho essentially annex southern and eastern Oregon and northernmost California. Leave San Francisco and Portland to the blue-staters, they're saying. We're all likeminded red-staters. It is backwards logic.

I'm as guilty—or perhaps as gullible—of this cognitive over-simplification as the rest of the population. I will admit that I actually feel a moment of buoyancy as I pass the state line into New Mexico. There is nothing but a single sign and a continued barren vista, but I suddenly feel a smidgen less tense, a bit more sanguine, simply by crossing an arbitrary demarcation that only exists on paper. It's ridiculous and a bit disturbing. There should be a sniglet for that.

PEOPLE ARE SAYING

ROSWELL, NEW MEXICO

I have reached the land of yucca and tumbleweeds, lonely windmills and layered mesas. After my trek through Kansas and the Panhandle, it's nice to see that the Earth isn't actually flat—at least for most of us. But this drive, in particular, also has become a reminder that America is mostly a land of unpopulated places. There are frequent signs along these ultra-rural eastern New Mexico roads: PASS WITH CARE. Are they joking? Nobody drives this way—almost literally. In some 70 miles since I headed south from Tucumcari, I have come across not a single car, not a single soul. It may be the most solitary stretch of road that I have ever encountered.

Not that I don't have company. An occasional grazing cow lifts its head, stops chewing, and watches me—utterly perplexed—as I zoom past. A coyote prances off the road and into the sagebrush, turning its head back toward me with a look of disdain. And every half-mile or so, I scare up a flock of birds, who dip and dart in front of Covfefe in a panic. It is repeatedly terrifying. I feel like I've spent most of the ride flinching, but I manage to avoid... well, most of them. There is a ghost town named Acme not far from where I'm headed, and I'm pretty sure one of the unlucky birds was a roadrunner. That might explain the look from the coyote.

Most depressing and revealing is the fact that everything I pass is abandoned. Hundred-year-old houses with collapsed roofs or windows blown out like empty eye sockets. Ancient automobiles rusting in overgrown fields. Little crossroads that may have once acted as settlements, but now sit ghostly silent and decaying. It is all positively post-apocalyptic.

Finally, U.S. 60 and a hint of activity. About a dozen miles later, at Fort Sumner, I rumble down a dusty road to a little outpost at a bend in the trail. It's the local chamber of commerce, such as it is, and its brick walls display paintings of a Who's Who of hooligans and the folks who brought them to justice. Calamity Jane. Doc Holliday. Old Man Clanton. Wyatt Earp...

A rooster crows in the distance, as I walk into a tiny cemetery containing a handful of gravestones. But only one marker is protected within a cage and shackled to cement at the feet of the deceased. It seems that folks have made off with this tombstone a couple of times before the shackles. Once, it was found in Texas; another time, in California. There's something about this one that captures the imagination.

BILLY THE KID
BORN NOV. 23, 1860
DIED JULY 14, 1881

Billy the Kid was a lot like a tumbleweed—detached from roots, bouncing from place to place, dropping its seeds as it rolls with the wind, leaving an often detrimental and even destructive record of its path. He was born—real name Henry McCarty—in New York City. Or maybe Indiana. Possibly Missouri or Kansas. His first run-in with the law came when he was about 14 and recently orphaned. He was caught stealing clothing from a Chinese laundry and then escaped the jailhouse by shimmying up a chimney. He became a roaming ranch hand, a gambler, a gang member, mostly a fugitive. After killing his first man during a dispute in an Arizona saloon, he adopted an alias—William Bonney—and quickly became known as "The Kid." He was still a teenager.

There exists a photograph, thought to be the only known photo showing Billy the Kid, which only further bolsters his mythology, like a snapshot of Bigfoot or the Loch Ness Monster. And when the subject has been elevated to legend, the implausible seems that much more plausible. There's the story, for instance, about how he was challenged to a showdown by a gunslinger named Joe Grant. Billy managed to obtain Grant's gun before the fight and make sure that an empty chamber was up first in the ill-fated man's revolver. Only Billy's gun went off. Of course, there's another version of the tale: It wasn't a showdown at all. Grant was terrorizing bar patrons, the Kid casually approached him and said, "That's a mighty nice-looking six-shooter you got." He spun its cylinder so that the next shot would be an empty chamber and handed it back. Later, when Grant tried to shoot Billy in the back... nothing. Billy shot him dead. Is either version true? Unlikely. But it fed the legend.

Billy was finally captured in New Mexico by legendary Sheriff Pat Garrett. He was found guilty and sentenced to hang for the murder of another sheriff in Lincoln, New Mexico, the site of a five-day firefight, part of the famous "Lincoln County War." Billy was all of 18 at the time—and may have killed at least that many men. The story goes that the judge sentenced him to hang until "you are dead, dead, dead." Billy responded, "And you can go to hell, hell, hell." And then improbable—perhaps impossible—events played out that seem Hollywood-scripted: He secretly slips out of his handcuffs during a trip to the outhouse, ambushes a guard, shoots the man to death with his own pistol, guns down a second guard, removes his leg shackles with a pickaxe, takes control of the courthouse, collects an arsenal of weapons, flees on a stolen horse... and becomes the West's most wanted man. And... scene.

Indeed, he became a celebrity in his own time—and that bled into historical remembrance as facts were reimagined through a sort of folk-hero lens. His legend has been nourished and romanticized by dime novels, songs, plays, and poems. The first film about him appeared in 1911, a silent movie that has been followed by more than 50 others—starring Roy Rogers, Paul Newman, Emilio Estevez, Val Kilmer. He was, one might argue, a serial killer, but there have been restaurants and roadside parks named for him. Tomorrow, I'll actually be driving through Lincoln, New Mexico, which is along a highway known as the Billy the Kid Trail, not far from the Billy the Kid Casino. Can you imagine a Son of Sam Parkway in Yonkers?

Billy the Kid finally met his demise when Garrett again tracked him down to the Maxwell Ranch in New Mexico. That tale: While Billy was gone, Garrett waited in the dark of a bedroom. When Billy returned, Garrett shot him in the heart.

Or did he? Rumor is the seed of conspiracy theory; myth is the manure that helps it grow. So it was with Billy the Kid.

He didn't die; Garrett shot the wrong man in the dark. Didn't his victim have a full beard? Billy had peach fuzz. So Garrett simply buried his mistake. No wait, Garrett didn't want to kill him at all; he actually helped the outlaw fake his death. Billy lived to be an old man under the alias "John Miller." No, that wasn't his alias at all—it was William Henry "Brushy Bill" Roberts, a fellow who emerged decades later and claimed to be Billy the Kid, right up to the moment he died of a heart attack at age 90 while walking to the post office in Hico, Texas.

As so often happens, there is a mass market for gullibility. So there is actually a Billy the Kid statue in Hico, along with a Billy the Kid Museum that tells the story of how Brushy Bill proved his identity by showing the wounds and scars on his body that exactly matched those of The Kid. Why would a fugitive's scars be widely known? Shrug. Yet Brushy Bill's story gained support over the years. He is buried near Hico, and plenty of visitors honor him by leaving bullet casings at his grave.

Billy the Kid's non-death is hardly the first American conspiracy theory. The tendency to see plots and hoaxes everywhere is as American as apple pie and Salem witch trials. Before the nation was even into its teens, religious leaders in New England were claiming that a secret organization called the Bavarian Illuminati was plotting to abolish Christianity and destroy the republic—with the help of Thomas Jefferson's political party. A few decades later, Samuel Morse, the inventor of the telegraph, published a book of his own conspiracy theories. A generation after that, the Know Nothings—so aptly named—promoted the idea of Irish refugees as Papist invaders and became America's first anti-immigration party. Sort of the way Trump used birtherism and anti-Mexican fearmongering to launch his political career and presidential campaign.

We are the United States of Conspiracy Theories. Some of them are harmless, like the notion that New Coke was briefly offered just to make old Coke taste better by comparison. A great many are simply irrationalities shouted by a segment of the paranoid populace. Bar codes? A satanic conspiracy. Jet plane contrails? Poison being spread by the government. The 1969 moon landing? Faked by NASA and Hollywood. But some—for instance, the Red Scare of the 1950s—have widespread and tragic repercussions. Senator Joseph McCarthy imagined a "conspiracy so immense and an infamy so black as to dwarf any previous venture in the history of man." As a result, he destroyed reputations and careers and lives.

However, that used to be an anomalous American experience. For the most part, wild postulations were generally the playground of fringe voices. But we have crossed a threshold. Political polarization has allowed emotion to influence how we interpret information. Outside actors like Russia have gleefully sown confusion. Social media has allowed light-speed propagation of crank theories and manipulatory memes, refracted through self-selected partisan filters. Truthiness is now deemed good enough. As a result, a huge swath of American voters has lost the ability to distinguish fact from fiction. Wanna-believers look for conspiracies. They weave them together into larger schemes.

They dismiss inconvenient evidence as having been planted, so that it only bolsters their worldview.

Conspiracism has become a belief system, as evidenced by a president who is both symptom and spreader, an instigator who peddles debunked piddle to his Twitter followers and who has turned the Oval Office into a bizarre echo chamber of paranoia.

A sign in Hico, Texas, informs folks that "many people believe" Brushy Bill Roberts was Billy the Kid. Trump's version is: "People are saying..." Pretending to passively pass on the latest gossip, he veers into wild, self-inflating fantasies targeted at his perceived enemies. "I retweet things and we start dialogue and it's very interesting," he once said. "Let people make their own determination." Or consider this bit of gutless accusation, regarding Vince Foster's death and the notion that the Clintons leave a trail of dead bodies: "I don't bring it up because I don't know enough to really discuss it. I will say there are people who continue to bring it up because they think it was absolutely a murder. I don't do that because I don't think it's fair."

Among the idiocies encouraged by Trump in his diarrhetic ramblings and retweets are the following:

Climate change is a Chinese hoax. Asbestos risks are a con. Obama was ineligible to be president. So was Marco Rubio. Ted Cruz's father palled around with Lee Harvey Oswald. It was somebody else's voice on the *Access Hollywood* tape. Widespread voter fraud caused him to lose the 2016 popular vote. Antonin Scalia may have been murdered ("I'm hearing it's a big topic. It's a horrible topic but they're saying they found the pillow on his face...") Vaccines can cause autism. Muslims in New Jersey cheered when the World Trade Center fell. Democrats inflated the Puerto Rican death toll from Hurricane Maria. Syrian refugees could be ISIS terrorists, as was a man who charged the stage at one of his rallies ("What do I know about it? All I know is what's on the internet.") Obama wiretapped his Trump Tower phones. A cybersecurity company named Crowdstrike framed Russia for election interference. The Obama Administration covered up a plot to stage Osama bin Laden's death.

All of this would be disturbing if it came from your local barbershop, let alone from the bully pulpit. When this delusional man wears a MAGA hat, it's irritating; but when he wears his tinfoil hat, it's dangerous. A president's attitudes shape the national narrative, and when he plays to the paranoia of his... let's call them a "basket of gullibles"... there are consequences.

When Trump called into Alex Jones's InfoWars show during the 2015 presidential campaign and told him, "Your reputation is amazing. I will not let you down," he was validating a villainous scumbag who re-terrorized families by claiming that the Sandy Hook shootings were an elaborate hoax staged to introduce strict gun control laws. When people in Trump's orbit, including the son of his first national security advisor, retweeted a Pizzagate conspiracy that placed Hillary Clinton at the center of an international child-sex-trafficking ring run out of a D.C. pizza joint, it didn't just disappear into the ether. It led one dupe to drive 360 miles and show up at the restaurant with an AR-15.

When an unfounded rumor emerged about George Soros funding Mexican caravans, and Trump tweeted that he "wouldn't be surprised" if it were true, he wasn't just passing on harmless twaddle. No, he was perpetuating a centuries-old conspiracist tradition of casting Jews as master manipulators; he was providing fodder for the New World Order theory that a group of international elites is controlling global events; he was probably lifting the spirits of the wackadoodles who think Denver International Airport stands above an underground city which serves as a headquarters of that shadowy organization. Of course, Trump prefers a national version of that drivel—the so-called "deep state," an entrenched and sinister bureaucracy of leftist politicians, leakers and intellectuals pushing an agenda to undermine his administration and destroy American values. Polls shows that roughly half the country has bought into the notion.

On a single day in December 2019, Trump posted 20 tweets from accounts that have promoted QAnon, the conspiracy theory that holds that Trump is working tirelessly to thwart a satanic cabal of corrupt world leaders led by the denizens of that "deep state." In another era, this ludicrousness—with its shadowy leader, cryptic riddles and cliché ominousness ("I've said too much")—would have been properly mocked and consigned to the periphery of American culture. But in the Trump era, QAnon is a bona fide movement—with literature and merchandising and dozens of 2020 congressional candidates who embrace it. It has been described as not just a conspiracy theory, but the birth of an extremist religion. It has been identified by the FBI as a potential domestic terrorism threat.

So what does Trump say about QAnon followers, ten weeks before the election? "I understand they like me very much, which I appreciate. I have heard that it is gaining in popularity... I've heard these are people that love our country." When a reporter pointed out that QAnon adherents believe that Trump is secretly saving the world from a satanic cult of pedophiles and cannibals, he replied, "Is that supposed to be a bad thing? ... If I can help save the world from problems, I'm willing to do it."

We have reached a terrifying tipping point.

———————

A few days ago, I passed through the little Ozarks hamlet of Goodman, Missouri. There wasn't much to it, except for an establishment called the Redneck Catfish Buffet. But I found neither rednecks not catfish, only the taste of disappointment. It was closed. So I filled up on gas instead at the Goodman Mini-Mart next door. As I topped my tank, a portly fellow in a stained gray T-shirt walked out with a pre-wrapped sandwich in one hand. Ron from Goodman was friendly enough. But as we started a conversation, he moved in a bit too close.

"Hold on," I began, as I fumbled with my face covering.

"Yeah, I saw your plates. I figure you guys don't have as much freedom as we do."

Uh-oh. California-bashing in the first round. "What do you mean?"

"Don't you guys have to wear masks everywhere you go?"

"Well, I want to. To be safe. You feel differently?" Can o' worms...

"Oh yeah. I just feel like the scientists aren't telling us the truth. They want us to get the vaccine. They want to make us want the vaccine. They're trying to scare us into begging for it. Otherwise, why would we allow a vaccine that hasn't been tested? If they're not trying to rush it, it should take five to seven years. They have to have an agenda, or why would they do that?"

And so it began.

Some of the most enduring conspiracy theories tend to develop during societal crisis situations, particularly unexpected catastrophes. It is a means of digesting a tragic event. Locating a complex cause offers a version of comfort, as opposed to accepting a mere accident of fate or an unsatisfying solution. Thus JFK assassination theories still echo decades later, and 9/11 conspiracies abound. There was advanced knowledge of the attacks. The U.S. air defense stood down to let the planes reach their targets. It was an inside job, a controlled demolition, a collaboration with al-Qaeda, a frame job. Flight 93 was shot down by a U.S. fighter jet. There were no planes at all, just missiles surrounded by holograms made to look like planes. And of course, the usual blame-the-Jews crew alleged that there was not a single Jewish victim and therefore the attacks must have been the work of the Mossad. Of course, hundreds of Jews actually died. One of them, sadly, was a college pal of mine whose wife was seven months pregnant.

If there are inconsistencies involved in a crisis, if the evidence leaves some room for ambiguity, conspiracy often fills the void. Thus COVID. Health crises have long been fodder for conspiratorial ideas, from HIV/AIDS to SARS, or the anti-vaxxer movement. The latter, predictably, is yet another Trump transgression: "I've seen it," he claimed during a primary debate, "a beautiful child, went to have the vaccine... a week later got a tremendous fever, got very, very sick, now is autistic." Unfortunately, beliefs can drive behavior. In the past decade, about 10 percent fewer parents have vaccinated their children. So when Trump used the word "hoax" to describe anyone who would dare call out his appalling response to the pandemic, it opened the door to the questioning of all things COVID. Add to that a confusing array of early misinformation about the virus, a documentary promoting conspiracy theories that received eight million views in a single week before being blocked by social media sites, and a global spread for which the only answer seems to be a worldwide vaccine, and guys like Ron from Goodman begin to fear that hidden forces are at work.

"Population control. Mind control," he explained. "You know Bill Gates is heading all this up, right?"

Sigh. If there is one kooky conspiracy theory that I most roll my eyes at, it's the notion that Bill Gates—who has spent most of his fortune in an effort to save lives around the globe and who donated $100 million to COVID treatment and research—is secretly aiming to make a killing and mess with our minds. It's just so profoundly irrational on so many levels. And, of course, a recent survey revealed that about 28 percent of Americans believe it.

"Yeah. I don't buy that." I wanted to scream it.

"He's not denying any of it," Ron insisted. Well, except for this headline from CNBC ten weeks earlier: "Bill Gates denies conspiracy theories that say he wants to use coronavirus vaccines to implant tracking devices."

"Seven billion people to get his vaccine—"

"But he already has a hundred billion dollars..."

"—and when you get the vaccine, we don't know what all's in it. It ties in with the 5G."

"The what?"

"5G internet. The wavelength. They're gonna be able to use that as a weapon against us. There's a lot of information out there." He inched closer. "Have you researched Agenda 21?"

I felt like a character in a spy movie. Maybe *Get Smart*. "What's that?"

"I'll just leave it to you. Agenda 21. Just research it."

Agenda 21, it turns out, is a generation-old non-binding UN resolution that suggests ways for governments and NGOs to promote sustainable development. Conspiracists view it as the cornerstone of a plot to subjugate humanity under an eco-total-itarian regime.

"But how do you know any of this is real? I mean it's all..." I decided not to mince words. "... conspiracy theory."

"Well... when you see... the documents are out there. You're free to check it out on your own. If you don't believe it, you don't believe it."

Here, of course, is one of the primary appeals of wild and convoluted theories to conspiracists. They find comfort in cherry-picking information and believing they see through deceptions that others ignore. It makes them think they're smarter than everyone else, when they're actually overwhelmingly misinformed.

"So you think COVID isn't real?" I asked this a few feet away from a newsstand in which the *McDonald County Press* headline was COVID-19 DEATHS INCREASE. Then Ron made what seemed like a tangential turn, but wasn't.

"Okay, here's a question for you. Are you a Christian?"

Oh boy. The foundations of the cult of conspiracism and spiritual belief are essentially one and the same: We want an explanation for the unexplained. I'm not sure how Ron expected me to answer, but he likely didn't expect me to blurt out an immediate "No." Imagine if he knew that I was actually part of a massive Jewish conspiracy...

"Book of Revelations. In the Bible. It's coming true right now. There is so much stuff happening right now that shows we are right at the beginning of Tribulations. So... my suggestion. First of all, I pray for you—that God will speak to you. 'Cuz this is important. I mean, Hell is real. Heaven is real. The consequence of not accepting Christ is real. Okay? So my challenge to you would be to pick up a Bible, pray for discernment when you read it."

Let me emphasize that: Ron, who believes COVID is a hoax dreamed up so a billionaire can implant microchips to track our movement, asked me to be discerning about what I read.

"I'd be happy to talk to you about Christ..." As he said it, he noticed my reaction. Half my face is masked, but the eyes are the window to the soul. "I kind of feel like you don't want to."

"No," I replied. "I'm good."

"Okay, well, people are going to say they're good until it's too late—"

"But that doesn't answer the question: Is COVID real?"

He scratches his salt-and-pepper goatee. "COVID's basically maybe a little more than a common cold. They're scaring and hyping people up to running to the doctor, getting tested, and the test actually is checking for a chromosome. Everybody has it. It's a miracle that anybody tests negative."

This is a bastardization of the facts. But move over, Dr. Fauci. Ron at the Mini-Mart knows better. "What about the two hundred thousand people who have died?"

"I don't believe the number. There are fewer people who die from COVID than would die from the flu every year—"

"That's not true. No more than fifty thousand people have died from the flu in a typical year. Nearly four times as many have died from COVID in six months, and that's with lockdowns and—"

"Again, that depends if you believe the information. I believe it's propaganda to scare us to go beg for the vaccine."

"But why would they want to do that? Why would they want to destroy the economy and—"

"So the elite can take over. Agenda 21. It all fits right in out of the Book of Revelations. I tell ya, it just lays it out."

He said it so matter-of-factly. Like it's a matter of fact. I tried a different tact. "Let me ask you this: What if you're wrong?"

"If I'm wrong?" He seemed taken aback, as if the possibility never occurred to him. "Okay, if I'm wrong, and COVID is real, and I die from it... I'm still going to go to Heaven and be with Christ."

Well, that's fucking great. "What if you give the virus to someone else, and it kills them?"

"Well, I guess my thought is..."

I never got an answer because at that moment another unmasked fellow walked up. He had a David Crosby mustache, a Kenny Rogers beard, and a Joe Walsh voice. "Is this guy bothering you?" He pointed to Ron, who laughed and explained to the man—his name was Ed—the nature of our debate, concluding with, "If they didn't have an agenda, wouldn't it take five to seven years to get a vaccine?"

"Well, the agenda," I pointed out, "is to stop people from dying."

"If you believe the numbers, and you do, which you are free to. I happen to not." He turned to Ed. "Do you believe the numbers?"

"Man, I don't know," Ed shrugged. "I'm confused about the whole thing. I mean, I'm respecting social distancing. When I go to Walmart, employees are wearing their masks, so out of respect I wear mine because I don't want people to be afraid of me, you know? And I've personally lost people. The head pastor and four others down in Monark Springs came down positive. His wife passed away from it. I have another friend, and his wife passed away from it. And I have three other friends who had a hard battle with it. So I mean, is coronavirus here? Yes it is. It's here. And I can't believe what I've been seeing. Have you seen what's going on? Today, a third person from that wedding in Maine came down with it. I mean the eighteen- to thirty-three-year-olds are going crazy with this stuff. Partying. And then later, people start dropping dead. So I don't know... I do know people are dying. And me and Ron have been good friends for a very long time, and we just agree to disagree."

I was struck not by Ed's sober perspective, but rather the fact that he expressed it with such reluctance. *I'm confused about the whole thing.* There are honestly parts of the country where the white noise of conspiracy has muffled the sound of sanity, where it somehow takes courage simply to accept the reality of a once-a-century health crisis.

There was a pause in the conversation. I adjusted my mask. Ron looked down at his sandwich. Then Ed added this: "You know, we're both city councilmen. You're looking at half the council here."

So there's that.

If there were a Mount Rushmore of American conspiracy theories, what would be on it? This is a tough one. One of my favorite moments of all-time was when Buzz Aldrin slugged a moon-landing denier. But... let's see, the JFK assassination, certainly. The Red Scare, too, because of the damage done. And I think COVID-is-a-hoax has chiseled its way in as well, for the same tragic reason. That leaves one spot, and it makes sense to include an iconic example of how a fantasticality can endure and transcend and take on a life of its own.

So I'm off to Roswell.

The tale begins on June 14, 1947, some 80 miles north of Roswell, when a rancher and his son were driving across their ranchland and encountered "a large area of bright wreckage made up of rubber strips, tinfoil, and rather tough paper, and sticks." They collected the wreckage, drove it all into Roswell, and handed it over to the local sheriff, who was just as perplexed as they were. The sheriff contacted a commander at the Roswell Army Airfield, who contacted his superior in Texas, who sent out an officer from the base to investigate more thoroughly. The Army didn't want to reveal a top-secret project at the time—an attempt to detect sound waves generated by possible Soviet atomic bomb tests by using microphones flown on high-altitude balloons. So the investigating officer put out an alternative statement instead. Thus the *Roswell Daily Record* ran a story that included this sentence: "The intelligence office of the 509th Bombardment Group at Roswell Army Air Field announced at noon today that the field has come into the possession of a Flying Saucer."

The very next day, the *Roswell Dispatch* posted a contradictory report. It was just a weather balloon. But the headline was telling: "Army Debunks Roswell Flying Disc as World Simmers with Excitement." This was a few years before the term "UFO" was even in the lexicon, but there was a bit of mass hysteria regarding "flying saucers"—more than 300 such sightings were reported in just the last six months of 1947. The Roswell story faded for a few decades, but eventually a global UFO industry began to emerge.

Seven years after the "crash," the Air Force had begun conducting "dummy drops," which involved dropping crash test dummies from high-altitude weather balloons. They looked waxy, often green-gray. Over the years, people began to conflate events while misinterpreting them. When it was revealed that the Army had, indeed, covered up its nuclear test-monitoring project, rumors only grew. No, there were two spaceships! There were little green men aboard! There was an alien autopsy! All of those off-limits government properties? They housed aliens, dead or imprisoned. "No Trespassing" signs became invitations for speculation, and hoaxers saw an opportunity. Four whole decades later, a Roswell mortician claimed that he had received a series of phone calls from the Roswell air base in 1947 asking how best to preserve small bodies and that a panicked nurse at the base had told him about three alien corpses that she saw there.

By then, hundreds of people claimed connection with the old "Roswell incident." Books, articles, TV shows... the prevailing zeitgeist breathed new life into the conspiracy theory. In 1995, a film purporting to show footage of the actual alien autopsy aired throughout the world. When it was revealed as a hoax a decade later, that got less attention. A couple of prominent skeptics have even coined a process—the "Roswellian syndrome"—by which a myth becomes a sort of phenomenon. They cited five stages of development: incident, debunking, submergence, mythologizing, and reemergence and media bandwagon effect. It is a blueprint for the evolution of a conspiracy theory.

Thus a nearly forgotten happening in rural New Mexico evolved into perhaps the world's most famous, most investigated—and discredited—UFO case. But it sure has been good for Roswell.

It was once a typical southwestern settlement. Originally just a couple of adobe buildings, it grew to become the sixth most populous city in New Mexico. There is a historic district. You can tour the ruins of the old Roswell Mill, a covered bridge, and some antebellum homes. But those aren't why people trek to Roswell. This city of some 48,000 earthlings has indeed been invaded—reinvented into an enclave for all things alien, a sort of municipal symbol of how conspiracy theories can blossom and dominate.

Roswell has chosen eccentricity over anonymity. It hosts a UFO Festival every July during which extroverts converge dressed as extraterrestrials. The city's civic seal depicts a visitor from outer space. The welcome signs at either end of town feature flying saucers, and Main Street is overrun by little green men—at the entrance to several motels, at the Shamrock gas station, at a used car lot. There's a green figure wearing a nurse's cap in the window of Frontier Home Health Services and another happily holding a scissors at Diamond Cuts barbershop. A half-mile up the street, a McDonald's is designed to look like a spaceship, and a 20-foot-tall, avocado-hued extraterrestrial holds up the "Dunkin' Drive Thru" sign. Main Street is bustling, as invaders from out of state wander among tourist traps—Alien Invasion, Alien Zone, a "blacklight adventure" called Spacewalk.

And, of course, the epicenter of all things alien—co-founded by that same opportunistic mortician four decades after the crash—is the International UFO Museum & Research Center, its name hoping to convey scope and seriousness. To my mind, it has about the same cache as International House of Pancakes. Signs at the entrance announce that they're limiting occupancy, requiring face coverings, screening every visitor's temperature. I do as they say and stare into a machine that tells me, "Temperature normal." As I peer into the museum, toward aliens, I'm hopeful that it's the last medical probe.

Then I embark on a trip into what the museum describes as a mission to "educate, not convince." Never mind the "Roswell... We Believe" mural painted on the building. So the section featuring old newspapers balances breathless headlines ("Saucer Outran Jet, Pilot Reveals") with somewhat apologetic ones ("Flying Disc Turns Up as Just Hot Air"). A display of "Photographic Evidence" of UFOs is followed by a wall dedicated to "Identified Flying Objects." The attitude ranges from tongue-in-cheek (*Star Wars* cut-outs) to tacky (silver-skinned aliens standing in front of a flying saucer).

As I hurry through the building—still mostly fearful of the COVID invasion—I'm trying to gauge how seriously the folks in Roswell take the fuss in Roswell. On the one hand, I'm creeped out by the image behind a glass wall that seems like some sort of dystopian Disneyland scene—a group of mannequins dressed as medical technicians autopsying a decomposing E.T. On the other hand, the "Little Bit of Humor" section features cartoons like the one showing two aliens strolling off a spaceship with golf clubs in hand.

Naturally, the tour ends at the gift shop, which actually offers tinfoil hats protecting against "alien and government mind control." You can buy camouflage caps ("Alien Hunter"), bumper stickers ("My other car is a UFO"), spaceship snow globes ("New Mexico or bust), and the obligatory "My family was abducted by aliens and all they brought me back was this crummy T-shirt." Roswell isn't really about conspiracies anymore; it's about capitalism.

I head to my campground, a few miles away at the eastern edge of town, thinking I've escaped the invasion, but I haven't. "Come crash with us!" shouts a Trailer Village sign. And sitting on a bench in front of the campground office, relaxed, satisfied, is a life-sized green extraterrestrial drinking a Bud Light and holding a thick joint.

If Roswell's goal was to entertain me, it succeeded. Persuade me? Nah. It was a damn balloon. There are no crashed saucers, no hidden aliens, no secret autopsies. You know why we can be certain? Trump.

This is a guy who invited the Russians into the Oval Office and disclosed classified information, revealed the always secret location of U.S. nuclear submarines to the president of the Philippines, gave away the location of Seal Team Five in Iraq by posting a video to Twitter, exposed sensitive military secrets because he tweeted a satellite photo to taunt Iran, and admitted—out loud—that if voting were made easier "you'd never have a Republican elected in this country again." He has no filtering mechanism whatsoever. President Tweetledum has gone so far down the rabbit hole that he genuinely trusts the *National Enquirer* more than *The New York Times*. So if some secret file informed him that there was, indeed, an alien autopsy conducted in Roswell in 1947, how long would it take for him to spew the information onto a rally stage? Twelve hours?

Then, of course, he'll move on to disseminating other self-obsessed imaginings: Ukraine is hiding Hillary Clinton's emails. A plane loaded with thugs is headed to the Republican Convention. MSNBC anchor Joe Scarborough once killed an intern. Windmills cause cancer. And every time he does it, I hear the echoes of that old joke about a friend who sent a postcard with a picture of Earth as seen from space. On the back it said, 'Wish you were here."

TESTED

A s I rumble out of Roswell, I figure it's the perfect plan. And we all know how that goes. I make a pit stop two hours west, and a theme starts to kindle. I'm in Capitan, home to Smokey Bear Historic Park.

Fictional Smokey Bear—as a symbol for fire prevention—was born on August 9, 1944, almost exactly between the birth dates of Biden and Trump, for what it's worth. The first poster showed Smokey, in what would become his traditional ranger hat and blue jeans, pouring a bucket of water on a campfire and saying, "Care will prevent 9 out of 10 fires." Within a few years, it was catchier: "Only YOU Can Prevent Forest Fires!", which later became "Only YOU Can Prevent Wildfires!" Somewhere along the line, folks began adding a "the" in the middle of his name. It's incorrect, like saying Mickey the Mouse.

But there was also a real Smokey Bear, a bear cub rescued from a burning forest here in the Capitan Mountains in 1950. He had climbed a tree to survive, but was badly burned. Sympathetic firefighters named him Smokey, and he became a bit of a phenomenon. He was moved to D.C.'s National Zoo. From there, he spread the word about wildfire prevention and forest conservation until his death in 1976. He's buried a few feet from where I'm parked.

Meanwhile, the world is on fire. Unprecedented warmer, drier conditions have doubled the number of large fires over the past few decades in the western United States. The world's five warmest years on record have occurred in the last five years, and as I left on this journey California was finishing up its hottest August ever. Sparked in part by a rare series of lightning storms, my home state has had a record wildfire year, with more than 8,000 blazes, some 4 million acres burned, 9,200 structures destroyed, 31 lives lost. Five of the six largest California wildfires in history are currently raging. Meanwhile Trump, if he talks about the fires at all (they're in blue states, after all), blames state governors and says only something along the lines of "I told them they should rake the floor." As usual, he has reduced a complex situation to narcissistic simplicity revolving around him knowing better than experts who have devoted their lives to studying such things. I saw a political cartoon today. It shows Smokey standing over a prostrate Trump, having just slugged him in the face: "It's climate change, you idiot."

Another hour or so, and I'm passing through scorched earth. About 5,000 years ago, 5,676-foot-tall Little Black Peak erupted here, sending a lava flow into the surrounding basin, creating 125 square miles of molten rock known as the Valley of Fires. The jumble of fissures and outcrops supports a surprisingly diverse ecosystem. Shrubs and desert grasses grow in the cracks. Cacti rise from the lava. Turkey vultures, golden eagles, and great horned owls swoop over the rugged landscape. Several four-legged species have developed a darker hue to match the black rock. Cataclysm comes, life goes on. Something to remember.

At mile marker 30 along Highway 380, I ease into a gravel pullout at the closest thing to a settlement that I've seen in a long while. You can't miss the sign. ROCK SHOP, it says. This is Bingham, New Mexico. In its entirety.

The co-owner, or at least the husband of the owner, is a fellow named Don. He's standing amid outdoor tables brimming with agates and jaspers and geodes. At first glance, my thoughts turn to a movie trope—when a nerdy protagonist accidentally knocks over a row of Harleys, and the angry owners march out of the biker bar. Don looks like he'd be the first one out. He's hefty, a former athlete, with a white goatee and gray hair past his shoulders. Intimidating. But he's in flipflops and cargo shorts, and he turns out to be an amiable guy.

"My wife's hot!"

Wait. What? All I asked was, "How'd you end up here?"

"She's hot! She's fourteen years younger. She wanted to live here." He shrugs, as if that was all the explanation needed. And maybe it is.

Don and I should have a lot to disagree about. He thinks COVID is a bit of a scam. There are bumper stickers adorning the walls of the Rock Shop that say things like PUT LOCKS ON CRIMINALS, NOT GUNS and EARTH FIRST!! WE'LL MINE OTHER PLANETS LATER. But instead we talk about sports ("Really?" I say. "The pitcher?" Turns out his brother-in-law is former major league all-star David Wells). We talk about names

("No shit?" he says. "My mother-in-law is a Herzog.") And we talk about The Bomb.

You see, tiny Bingham is the closest town to the Trinity Site—where the world's first atomic bomb was tested. At 5:29 a.m. on July 16, 1945, 16 miles south of Bingham, New Mexico witnessed a blast so powerful that it shattered windows 120 miles away and left a crater eight feet deep and 1,200 feet across. One observer described it as a desert sun appearing in the middle of the night. I suppose it was the time and place at which Americans convinced themselves of the efficacy of total annihilation. I glance south and spot a couple of low clouds in the distance. Hard to believe that it was once a mushroom cloud.

"Softball-sized chunk of uranium. Compressed to the size of a paperclip," Don says, as he shows me photographs inside the Rock Shop. "And then..." He makes an explosion noise.

Don points to one of the rarer rocks for sale—Trinitite. Essentially, it is sand melted into glass by the explosion. Nuclear glass. I'm tempted to take one home, but it's shockingly expensive. And I prefer my keepsakes to be less radioactive.

Later, as I'm leaving, I ask him, "So Bingham... population two?" Don and his hot wife live in a double-wide behind the shop.

Don shakes his head. "Now it's four people. A guy bought the place down the road last August." He nods toward a little ranch a few hundred yards away. "I asked him why," Don adds. "Why would he want to come here?"

"What was his answer?"

"He said, 'Cuz the world is coming to an end.'"

So I have that ringing in my ears as I coast another 50 miles west to my second stop—the Very Large Array. It's... well, it's an array of very large dish antennas forming a super-powerful radio telescope that gathers invisible light—radio waves. The antennas are set up on tracks, moveable, often covering more than a hundred square miles of landscape. It is incredibly cool.

COVID has closed the visitor center to the public, but I drive down a gravel road far enough so that I can stroll next to one of the 27 giant dishes sitting many hundreds of yards apart. It is exhilarating to stand out in the open desert, not another soul in sight, alongside a massive piece of technology that has been said to have made more discoveries than any other telescope on Earth: how stars are born, how galaxies expand, the relentless power of black holes.

And yes, they search for signs of life out there. Of course, they needn't bother because, back in Bingham, ol' Don is on the job. He admitted, only half-joking, that he's been looking for aliens ever since he got there a couple of decades ago: "I figure that Roswell crash happened in '47. That was only two years after the bomb exploded. The aliens were probably like, 'Huh? What was that?'"

I climb back into Covfefe and aim toward the grand finale of my master plan. Forty-five miles more, and I'll be in a tiny hamlet called Pie Town. That's right. And a charming little restaurant there, now supposedly under new ownership, is called The Gatherin' Place. They specialize in pie. Adorable, right? I've been there before with my family, back when it was known as the Pie Town Café. Delicious.

I'm going to order takeout. Since I'm in New Mexico, a green chile cheeseburger. And since I'm in Pie Town, how about a hefty slice of blueberry butterscotch. Then I'm going to walk over to the Continental Divide just a few steps away and savor the goodness as the sun sets magnificently over a nation's backbone.

Perfect.

I slice through the Datil Mountains in western New Mexico, elevated, anticipating. There it is, at the crest of a hill. Pie Town.

And then my heart drops. This hiccup of a place feels bleak, like a bike left to rust by the side of the road. The only life seems to be the gathering at The Gatherin' Place. I park a few steps away, grab a mask, and prepare to eat well for the first time on this excursion and trade small talk with some locals in Stetsons, all of us a-gatherin'.

But I stop a dozen feet short. There, flapping boldly in the wind above the entrance, are a couple of large and familiar flags— the first that I've seen, oddly enough, since central Kansas.

TRUMP 2020—KEEP AMERICA GREAT

TRUMP 2020—NO MORE BULLSHIT

Sigh. I drop my head in disappointment. I can't. I just can't.

Several moments pass as I struggle with a moral dilemma, a remarkable moment that might have been unimaginable back when the American landscape seemed less like a case of white hats and black hats, when there were at least shades of gray. And then...

Screw this creepy town. I continue another 70 miles into Arizona, where I microwave a breakfast sandwich for dinner.

I'M WITH STUPID
SHOW LOW, ARIZONA

I didn't pass my first pro-Biden sign until just before I reached Kentucky's Land Between the Lakes. It was only about a couple square feet in size, and I was speeding by, but I'm pretty certain I saw it in a front yard on the other side of Highway 68, which felt like spotting an albino bison.

The second one was in southern Illinois. I'd been passing Trump signs for several miles. Then I turned onto State Highway 37 toward the southernmost tip of the state, where the blue waters of the Ohio River join up with the brown waters of the Mississippi, creating a powerful visual metaphor for America's demographic circumstances. In fact, I'd argue that either the fear or support of that confluence is what motivates Americans on either side of the ideological spectrum. For what it's worth: The brown Mississippi proves the stronger of the two. The second Biden sign was a bit north of there, near Mound City, where more than 8,000 veterans are buried in a ten-acre national cemetery.

The third one was on the outskirts of Pocahontas, Arkansas—a front yard containing three old cars, a boat, and a VOTE BIDEN sign. I saw the fourth in Winfield, Kansas. The fifth, hanging from a rancher's fence, was on the outskirts of Lincoln, New

Mexico: BIDEN/HARRIS 2020... TRUTH MATTERS. It got to the point where I would raise a fist and whoop each time I saw one, depressingly giddy over the fact that someone was able to tell a statesman from a con man.

And that's it. Five. A cross-country drive. Five.

I've counted 71 Trumps banners and signs. TRUMP 2020... TRUMP/PENCE FOR VIRGINIA... GOD. GUNS. COUNTRY. TRUMP. But even those seemed to dematerialize once I was nearly halfway across the country. Probably, it was a product of the roads I chose and the scarcity of towns along the way. Possibly, my eyes were getting tired. Certainly, my middle finger was. I cruised 150 miles along Kansas highways before I noticed any national campaign signs. Plenty of local ones, though. Petersen for State Senate. Helmer for Kansas House. And, boy, if Ken White doesn't get elected sheriff, it's not for a lack of signage.

But still... 71-5.

It's as much a reflection of the rural, red-state path I've taken as anything, and it's probably not a legitimate harbinger of November's outcome. At least not entirely. But it does say something. Only, what exactly?

I have a theory. A Biden sign is a statement of support, but in more left-leaning parts of the world there are other options that convey passionately held beliefs. A declaration of worldview often takes different forms: BLACK LIVES MATTER... HATE HAS NO HOME HERE... THIS HOME EMBRACES DIVERSITY, EMPOWERS WOMEN, BELIEVES IN SCIENCE, KNOWS LOVE IS LOVE, FIGHTS INJUSTICE, WELCOMES IMMIGRANTS. But the other perspective counters that with the simple and tasteful: T-shirts that say "Fuck your feelings." Or its translation: "Vote Trump."

A Trump sign, often, is a statement of unconditional devotion—to a man, to a brand, to a team. It's like hanging a "Roll Tide" banner from your front porch, or affixing a Raiders Nation window decal to your Mustang, or wearing a Green Bay Packers cheesehead. During the 2016 campaign, Trump began to sound like Knute Rockne—if Knute Rockne were ineloquent and unhinged. "We're going to win so much, you're going to be so sick and tired of winning, you're going to come to me and go 'Please, please, we can't win anymore'... You'll say 'Please, Mr. President, we beg you sir, we don't want to win anymore. It's too much. It's not fair to everybody else.' And I'm going to say 'I'm sorry, but we're going to keep winning, winning, winning.'"

His acolytes believe he has done that. They're big fans. Growing up in Chicago in the '80s, I was a big fan of the Chicago Bears, which meant I celebrated their coach, Mike Ditka. Only later, through the lens of time and distance, have I come to realize that he's dumber than a cantaloupe. Ditka is a member of the "If you don't like it, get the hell out of the country" brigade. He probably has a Trump sign in his yard. So while the Trump phenomenon has been compared to reality television—for obvious reasons—it's more like pro wrestling or Sunday football. A large swath of America found a rooting interest. Never mind the particulars. You can bet the Patriots didn't lose fans after being caught cheating.

More than that, a Trump banner represents a big F.U. for the world to see. Or even not to see. Back in Kentucky, as I headed toward Science Hill, I found myself on a country road that immediately felt like a bad idea. It was barely wide enough for Covfefe—as long as nobody else came in the opposite direction. But I needn't have worried. The folks who live amid those cornfields must see no more than six cars a day. Of course, that didn't stop one of them from posting a sign—that same bullshit about no more bullshit.

Who is it meant for? Nobody. No one but the guy who owns the farmhouse. He's venting. He's telling you who he is. It's sort of like those old "I'm With Stupid" T-shirts that were popular back in the '70s, the ones with an arrow pointing to whatever poor schlub you're standing next to. The shirt always said far more about the wearer than the guy next to him.

That's what the Trump banners convey: I'm With Stupid. Actually, just a half-mile further that day in Kentucky, I passed a stark white house with only one adornment—a waving Confederate flag. I guess the allegorical arrow was pointing to him.

So I stopped being surprised by this myopic fandom—until I reached Show Low, Arizona.

A bustling outpost amid the White Mountains, Show Low was named for a card game. The story goes that in 1876 a couple of ranchers named Cooley and Clark each had claims for 100,000 acres of land. For some reason, they determined that two families couldn't share it. Each refused to buy the other out. So they played a game of Seven Up to settle the matter. Toward the end, Cooley needed just one point to win. Clark held a three of clubs. With nothing to lose, he said, "Show low, and you win the match." Cooley flipped his card. A deuce of clubs.

On Deuce of Clubs Avenue, the city's version of Main Street, there's a statue commemorating the moment. Not 20 steps away is a squat, blue-gray building—the color of an old Confederate uniform, actually. It looks like a former mechanic's garage. In fact, that's what it is. About 15 miles outside of town, I had passed a large white billboard. In big black letters it said only, "JESUS." And wouldn't you know, that's just what I mutter when I come across the ultimate in "I'm with Stupid." Right in the center of a town named Show Low on a street named for the lowest card in the deck, the Trumped Store.

I've been gathering questionable establishment names along this journey. Fast Eddie's Bait & Tackle and Restaurant in Fairdealing, Kentucky. The Hillbilly U-Pump gas station in Salem, Arkansas. Dust Bowl Bar & Grill in Dalhart, Texas. The Perk N Jerk coffee shop in Roswell. But Trumped? Why not call it the Conned Shop? Or the Duped Emporium? Surely, it has something to do with tiptoeing around trademarks. Not that Trump is litigious or anything.

I park across the street from the store—not alongside it, where a sign announces, "Reserved parking for deplorables only"—and I watch a procession of customers. They don't only come from Show Low, where registered Republicans outnumber Democrats 3 to 1. Some folks drive for hours just to buy a "Make Your Birthday Great Again" greeting card. Or a $25 Trump magnetic talking button ("All I can say is it's totally fake news. It's fake. It's fake."). Or a print that vomits: "The first time in history that a billionaire moves into public housing vacated by a Black family." Occasionally, a driver passes in a pickup truck, honking a horn in support. *Hey! Racism isn't a dealbreaker for me either! Go team!*

I move closer, and I notice the door is open at the store. Not figuratively, of course. I don a face covering—two, actually—and follow a beefy, bearded fellow into the store. Moments later, he's posing for a selfie like a fangirl—next to life-sized cardboard cutouts of the anti-immigrant president and his immigrant wife. A man sporting a stupendous mullet orders an espresso. They call it "freedom juice." I'm tempted to yank the barista's chain by ordering a vanilla latte. "I'll have a White Nationalist, please." Nearby, a young mother pushes a baby stroller. "I know! It's so cute!" she says. "They don't have it in his size." She stands near a pile of "Trumplican" onesies. It's like a bizarro Starbucks inside a dystopian Baby Gap.

A family of four marches into the store, the young boy and girl happily ripping off their masks as they enter. They look around, mouths agape, as if they're at a Disneyland gift shop. The boy makes his way to a table brimming with bumper stickers that offer Shakespearean turns of phrase like SUCK IT UP BUTTERCUP. TRUMP IS PRESIDENT and CAUTION: RIGHT-WING EXTREMIST ON BOARD. The boy chuckles and holds one up to his father. "You have to get this!" It says DADS AGAINST DAUGHTERS DATING DEMOCRATS. Later, as he walks out, that boy will turn to his mom and say, breathlessly, "That was probably the coolest store I've ever been in."

Apparently, the owners of this sewage plant ran northeastern Arizona's Trump campaign headquarters in 2016. They saw the demand for all things Trump, so after the election they signed a ten-year lease for the building, banking on Trump's reelection. Literally. You can purchase a bedazzled "Women for Trump" hat and a fly swatter featuring Trump's angry visage. They're even raffling off a framed lithograph of the iconic Washington-crossing-the-Delaware scene; only it's Trump instead. "Crossing the Swamp." Of course, half the people shown in Trump's boat—Bolton, Mattis, Kelly—have since called him dangerous to democracy.

A middle-aged woman picks up a CD for sale. "The Donald Trump Bump" must certainly rank among the worst songs ever written, right up there with Eddie Murphy's "Party All the Time." This one's more of a party-before-country tune, which has been warbled at Second Amendment rallies in front of the store. The lyrics will make your ears bleed: "All those accusations ain't worth a hill of beans... We finally got a president who says what he means... The liberals are mad. Can't believe their defeat... And all Trump really did was pull the covers and tweet..."

I need some air. So I sit on a bench in front of the store, pretending to work my phone. In reality, analogously, I'm pretending to be a Reds fan when I actually bleed Dodger blue. They don't take too kindly to the occasional do-gooders who think this spot along Deuce of Clubs is a fine place for a little demonstration on behalf of voter registration or sensible gun laws. One time, the owner heard a rumor that a busload of Black Lives Matter protestors was headed their way, so he had the American Guard stand watch over the store. You know the American Guard—the folks who believe the following: "An army from the south, emboldened by racist left wing propaganda stating the land was stolen by evil white people, pours into the country daily, financed by leftist welfare programs.

The goal? Total destruction of America, to be replaced by a new Marxist country known as Aztlan."

No protesters showed up, of course. There never were any. I'm With Stupid.

My civil disobedience alarm is sounding in my head. Should I do it? I'm tempted, so tempted, to grab a copy of my little *Dump Trump* book from Covfefe, waltz back into the store, and place on it on the table next to the talking toilet paper roll ("I will build a great, great wall!"). Maybe I'll open it to the page showing a wall of decency being built around Trump—bricks that say DIGNITY, HUMILITY, EMPATHY, INTEGRITY. Or maybe I'll show them their hero on the cover and ask if they'd like to sell my book at the store. Never mind that the drawing shows Trump following a sign that says "Karma" as he drives toward a cliff.

It would certainly make me feel better to make a scene. But then who would live to tell the story? I look up to see a sign— "Guns are Welcome on the Premises"—and good sense prevails.

In the window of the Trumped Store, there's another sign— wordy, lyrical in a way, something that might have been penned by the poet laureate of the Kingdom of Xenophobia: "We are not racist, phobic or anti whatever-you-are. We simply like here the way it is and most of us actually came here because it's not like there, wherever there was. You are welcomed here, but please stop trying to make here like there. If you want here to be like there, you should not have left there to come here, and you are invited to leave here and go back there at your earliest convenience."

In other words, as Trump once told a couple of congresswom- en, if you don't like it, go back to where you came from. Not happy here? Get the hell out.

So that's exactly what I do. I skip town so fast that I'm long gone while the saloon doors are still swinging. I travel south, down into the salmon-colored hills of Cedar Canyon, deep into the desert of Navajo County, to the lands belonging to proud people whose ancestors long predated those chest-beating half-wits at the Trumped Store. I'm just going to make an 80-mile loop through the Fort Apache Reservation, a drive to clear my head. A dose of reality, however bleak, to counter the manufactured retail version back in Show Low.

The Kinishba Ruins are first. A gravel turnoff from the highway, and a short hike to the sprawling remains of what was once a 600-room pueblo that housed as many as one thousand Zuni and Hopi natives. This was centuries ago. The collection of buildings was vacated long before Christopher Columbus took a wrong turn, called it a "New World" and classified the natives as "Indians." There should be a sign at the ruins: "If you want here to be like there, you should not have left there to come here, and you are invited to leave here and go back there at your earliest convenience."

The road through the reservation feels similarly abandoned. I quickly discover why. Signs along the avenue plead for safety. "COVID-19 is Real!"... "Stay at Home"... "No Visiting"... And finally, a declaration that explains the eerie quiet: "This Community is on a Self Initiated Lock-Down." Not 40 miles away, a couple of signs at the Trumped Store shout, "Face Masks NOT Required." The few people in the store who bother with so-called face coverings have them pulled below their noses, which is like placing a condom on your elbow.

Meanwhile, as I steer along South Chief Avenue, I find myself behind a white pickup truck. A young man, maybe 18 years old, sits in the bed of the truck. Pandemic fears here are such that he's not riding with the driver. He's strapped to a folding chair, all but his eyes hidden by a black face covering. He stares at me as I rumble a few dozen feet behind. It is a haunting image.

While the shoppers in Show Low revel in their God-given Right to Infect, the White Mountain Apache Tribe and the massive Navajo Nation just to the north are reeling from some of the highest COVID infection rates in the country. The Apaches have been infected at more than ten times the rate of the state as a whole. The virus took advantage of tribal strengths (often three or four generations living under one roof) and weaknesses—systemic poverty, food insecurity, high unemployment, lack of critical infrastructure.

There's an old Apache proverb: "It is better to have less thunder in the mouth and more lightning in the hand." While Trump mocked Pocahontas and washed his hands of any responsibility, tribal leaders mandated masks, extended curfews, and recruited a small army of contact tracers. They were successful in bringing the rate of cases down. A couple of days before my arrival, they even celebrated a day of no new COVID cases. But while Trumpers are buying T-shirts that declare, "In Trump We Trust," the Apache are focused on the practicalities of survival. I pass a marquee at the local Christian Church: "Stock up. Food and water. 14 days supply on hand."

Amid the juvenility of the Duped Emporium back in Show Low, I spotted a particularly infantile piece of merchandise: a windshield visor showing Trump and his third wife in the front seat of a car and a screaming baby strapped into a car seat in the back. The baby is Hillary Clinton. But while the knuckle-draggers are gloating about preservation of the glass ceiling, the White Mountain Apache Tribe and its 16,000 members have made history. Gwendena Lee-Gatewood, the youngest of eleven children, had been an executive assistant to the tribal chairman and had served as the tribe's public information officer. Last April, she was elected as the first-ever tribal chairwoman.

Her challenge, even putting COVID aside, is immense. The numbers are stark. In the WMAT, nearly one-third of households are headed by single mothers. The tribe's per capita income of less than $9,000 is three times lower than the state average. More than half of tribal members under the age of 18 are considered to be living in poverty. In fact, most of them are considered—by a ratio of income to poverty threshold—to be "severely poor." Maybe it's fitting that when I follow the "Tribal Headquarters" sign toward a couple of low-slung red-brick buildings, all I find is a weedy lot and a stray dog begging for food.

Covfefe is sputtering—more than ever today—as I continue north, finishing my loop. Past a roadside memorial alongside an abandoned playground—a cross, flowers affixed to a chainlink fence, a child's desk, and a teddy bear wearing a protective face covering. Past the tiny Whiteriver Indian Hospital, where a flag appears at half-mast. Past a couple of hitchhikers whom it pains me to snub. Finally, past the Hon-Dah Casino amid the ponderosa pines at the fringe of the tribal lands. "Hon-Dah" means "welcome" in Apache, but the casino is only beginning to reopen after being shut down for five months, costing the community millions of dollars in much-needed revenue.

And now I'm off the reservation, coasting through the sudden bustle of a couple of resort towns until I arrive back in Show Low, where "Trumped Headquarters" sells gold-plated $100 bills bearing the pancake-makeup-covered face of a failed casino magnate who once testified to a House subcommittee about competitor casino owners: "They don't look Indian to me."

At the entrance to the store, a balloon representation of the president gives a thumbs-up. Customers laugh and sip "freedom juice" and peek into their bag of new purchases. And the waving flags say, TRUMP 2020. KEEP AMERICA GREAT.

PERSPECTIVE
GRAND CANYON, ARIZONA

O ne final detour. If you're traveling within 80 miles of a global icon, you don't pass that up.

The drive from Flagstaff to Grand Canyon National Park proves to be the most harrowing of my journey—not because the road seems perilous (it is a well-paved delight through the ponderosas), but because Covfefe is struggling, surging and gasping for air even at 50 miles per hour, as if unable to find the proper gear. My ride is wheezing in front of a row of impatient drivers, and I have nowhere to catch my breath. There are few turnoffs—and no shoulder at all. I'm white-knuckling my way forward, well aware that it would just be so 2020 for Covfefe to die just miles short of a place on most everyone's bucket list.

I finally make it to my campground, seven miles south of the South Rim, as night falls. They put me in the cheap seats, the electric-only campsites where they obviously like to place the horse trailers, too. I'm parked among myriad mounds of manure—so much so that I decide not to marvel at the stars tonight for fear of stepping in a pile of shit. A cynic might find that symbolic.

But the next morning is glorious. I park in a near-empty lot and rush to the rim, performing what is surely a ritual that all

Americans have in common when arriving at one of the Seven
Natural Wonders of the World: Gasp. Gape. Grin. I'm gob-
smacked, as always, by this great cataclysm of the earth that
actually consists of too many canyons and colors to count, a rock
palette of rusty reds and dusty pinks, delicate greens and deep
maroons, slate-grays and all shades of brown. Ink-black ravens
swoop below me, yet far above the canyon floor. Tiny humming-
birds flit from branch to branch of the cedar trees that line the
rim wall. Squirrels scamper and dig, glance up with paranoid
eyes, then commence scampering and digging again. One waltz-
es up to within inches of me, stands on its hind legs, rubs two
tiny hands together, and gives me the most earnest expression I
have ever seen. But he's standing in front of the "Let the squirrels
feed themselves" sign. Location, location, location.

Nearly as gratifying as the view is the running first-glimpse
commentary. One couple in their early twenties reaches the rim
a dozen feet from me.

"Oh wow!" she exclaims. "Oh my god!"

"Epic as fuck!" he offers.

"Look at those rock formations. They almost look like they
were formed by man or something."

"Yeah, they were formed by *the* man."

"Or wo-man."

"Hey look, there's water down there!"

"That's a long way down."

"Man, this never gets old."

Of course, it's ancient. For five or six million years, the
Colorado River has been carving through rock some two billion
years old, forming a fissure in the earth 6,000 feet deep at its

deepest point and 18 miles wide at its widest. This sublime spectacle is the product of inexorability, incremental movement—the flow of water and the march of time. In an epochal battle between a rock foundation and a transformative stream, the river wins every time. But from the South Rim, even the chocolate-brown river is barely visible.

I can't help but glimpse a metaphor for this American moment that I've been trying to capture in words. Our country's massive divide didn't emerge overnight. The rift has been forming for ages, growing ever wider, yet we can never actually see it happening. Until we're there—a chasm revealing contrasting layers, each sliver of color representing countless years of pressure. Due to the minerals therein, each rock strata responds to the erosion of What Was in a different way. Defiant spires. Plunging slopes. Perilous outcroppings. Jagged edges. Folds and crevices that hold secret marvels and hidden threats. Glorious explosions of color. These features aren't created over time, so much as exposed.

A sixty-something couple in matching sweatsuits hurries by, looking like they just speed-walked from Scarsdale. "How many people do you think have died here?" she asks. He shrugs. She adds, "I bet that's something you can Google."

I know the answer because I have a dash of cremnophobia— the fear of cliffs. My admiration of the view is always somewhat spoiled by my anxiety about plummetous possibilities. To me, it's not a rim; it's a precipice. I'm always too well aware of the gravity of the situation. An average of 2.5 people each year fall to their deaths at the Grand Canyon. I guess I'm fearful of winding up as that .5, if you know what I mean. So I stay several feet from the edge, watching as two visitors scamper out to a precarious overlook that looks like something even Wile E. Coyote might avoid.

"What are they doing?" asks a young Latino boy nearby.

"Just looking," says his mom. "Appreciating. Meditating. Thinking."

To continue the allegory, the view of the divide changes dramatically with the whims of the weather and the time of day. A fading sun paints the divide in vivid hues. Clouds throw shadows over the spectacle. This view that I'm inhaling is only my perspective amid a certain climate at a particular time. But if anything, the Grand Canyon is a clarion call to linger, to revel in the moment before returning to the relative disappointment of the flat and featureless world beyond. Duly inspired, I amble along the rim trail for a few miles, purposeless, just looking and listening.

Generally, U.S. national parks are brimming with overseas visitors—nearly 15 million a year. But COVID has changed the dynamic. International travel mostly has been replaced by the old-fashioned road trip. Americans in need of an escape from sheltering in place have opted to flood into the open spaces, which may constitute one of those scarce silver linings—a nation rediscovering the marvels in its own backyard. So I stroll past a satisfying spectrum of humanity. And dogs. Lots of panting dogs.

A middle-aged tandem—his face is smothered in sunscreen—shuffles along the trail. "See," she tells him, "this is more my speed." An Indian-American couple discusses where they want to watch the sunset. A husband and wife speak German to each other from beneath matching floppy hats. A multi-generational group walks by, and I hear one of them say, "Yeah, it's getting down to the wire. But it might turn out okay. We can always stay at Dad's for a while..." A heavyset Black man pushes a wheelchair bearing an older white woman in a bedazzled shirt that implores: "Believe. Inspire. Impact." In the other direction, a young couple maneuvers a little girl in a stroller. Brooklyn—that's her name—shouts "Hi!" to every single person she passes. And every person responds with a genuine smile.

I sit for a spell on a bench near what appears to be an Amish family. An older father with a long, white, mustache-less beard and his young son wear matching hats. Two daughters stand nearby, curiously and nervously surveying the scene. I wonder where they come from, how they got here. Everywhere, people are posing for pictures, unnaturally in a natural wonder, including one father and his five children perched dangerously on the edge of an outcropping while the mother snaps a photo from an overlook a hundred feet away. A Latina woman walks by and shakes her head. "Oh, hell no!" She notices me smiling in agreement, and we share a chuckle.

Here, the differences among us seem more communal than adversarial. Some people keep their distance from one another; others decidedly don't. Many people are masked; equally as many aren't at all. But it is a refreshingly judgment-free atmosphere, in an escaping-reality kind of way. If folks wore their politics on their sleeves here, the vibe would be entirely different. The façade of shared wonder would dissolve. You can't enjoy the view when you're giving someone the side-eye. But the only hint of that is a man of about 70 in a black T-shirt that declares: "I stand for the flag. I kneel for the cross." He and his wife are scanning a park map, turning it this way and that. "Oh, I thought we were way over here," she says. It's a one-direction trail, and they're lost.

As I make my way back toward my starting point, I pass an N95 dropped on the trail, and my imagination conjures up various stories inspired by the mysterious artifact. I hear a loud voice piercing the general quiet, and I arrive at Mather Point Amphitheater—a stone ampitheater handcrafted from local limestone—to find an extended African American family gathered in joyful celebration. One woman adorned in head-to-toe tie-dye has matching rainbow hair braided all the way down past her ankles. Another wears a black sweatshirt with white lettering: CHANGE. They've brought their own music, and they're blasting it. While I hate the intrusion of sound, I actually like the song, so I look it up. It's a French neo-soul duo called HER—childhood pals, one of whom succumbed to cancer not long after the release of their debut album. That knowledge lends profundity to the lyrics: "All I need is five minutes... If you can see the signs... All I need is five minutes... If you read between the lines..."

I return to the parking lot, and I encounter a man who most certainly isn't wasting his five minutes. Greg Rasanen's eyes are barely visible between his face covering and his iconic National Park Service Ranger straw hat, but I recognize him as the friendly guy who welcomed me at the park entrance. I start our brief conversation with an observation about the array of visitors who have flocked to the canyon.

"Despite political and cultural differences, everybody does appreciate both nature and its grandeur," he nods. "Across

America, everybody would generally agree that national parks are an amazing thing that we have. Both ends of the political spectrum have an appreciation for them."

"Not necessarily both ends of the people making the decisions." Typical me. Glass half-empty.

"Yeah, yeah. The two ends probably have different perspectives on how to manage them."

I nod. There's a momentary lull. So I turn to the question that I've asked often along this excursion: "Tell me... how'd you end up here?" You'll recall that Don at the rock shop in Bingham, New Mexico, offered a line about his wife being hot. Stefan at the store in Appomattox launched into a Long-Island-to-rural-Virginia tale that was more witness-protection than wanderer. The militia crew playing dress-up in Harrison, Arkansas, basically just showed me their guns.

"So..." Greg begins, "I have a bucket list of adventure jobs. That's what I've been doing with my life. Park ranger was on the list. So I've been doing this for a little over a year now. This is my third park. It's been great because I've bounced around the country. Started out in the Black Hills of South Dakota at Wind Cave. When down to Castillo de San Marcos in St. Augustine, Florida. Now I'm here for a season. I'm getting to see the country and the parks and dive into the history of each place."

Greg grew up in Green River, Wyoming, which is where John Wesley Powell began the last great exploration of unknown territory in what became the continental U.S.—a century-and-a-half ago with ten men in four awkward, wooden boats. He eventually reached the Colorado River and the Grand Canyon. But I might argue that Greg's journey to the same place has been equally audacious. He joined the military at age eighteen and has been bouncing from adventure to adventure ever since.

"I was in the Army for ten years," he explains. "Did field artillery, armor, military intelligence. Then I got out and worked at a ski resort in Breckenridge. Then I went back and worked with DARPA, the Defense Advanced Research Projects Agency, and basically traveled around the United States, Afghanistan, and Iraq, training soldiers on a new software program. And then I jumped straight over to South Korea as an English teacher. Then I went up to Alaska and worked on a crabbing boat. And then to Florida where I worked in the yachting industry. I was a deck hand, so I worked on everything from the mega yachts to sailing yachts to sport fish boats. Did that for a couple of years up and down the East Coast, the Caribbean, the Pacific...."

"So you literally have a list?"

"Yeah, it's changed over time. Meeting people, learning about different jobs, I'll add stuff. And then getting too old for things, I'll take stuff off. When I was a younger man, being a smoke jumper was on there. But I'm forty-four now."

"So what's next?" Skydiving instructor? Safari guide? Storm chaser?

"The next two jobs on the list are... a winery—follow the grapes from vine to bottle... and a flight attendant on a small charter aircraft."

My younger son once had a bucket list of his own that he taped to the wall next to his bed when he was about 11 years old. Along with "visit Hawaii" and "go to Paris," his list included "jump out of a moving car" and "eat fish and chips." We all have our own thresholds for aspiration and adventure. Risk is relative, and exotic is in the eye of the beholder. Anyway, what impresses me about Greg the Ranger-Soldier-Trainer-Teacher-Crabber-Deck Hand is not what he's done, but why.

"Basically, I was looking at either a career in the Army or getting out. There were two schools of thought: One was either save your whole life and work hard and do the things you want to do when you retire. And the other was... the world's coolest jobs, and doing things where you basically get paid to experience the world. I decided to take that route."

I might have experienced a twinge of self-doubt upon meeting a positively peripatetic person like Greg. While he's been traversing the globe, patrolling black diamond runs, and battling blue marlin, I've been comfortably meandering through the American atlas, all the while headed toward home, and picturing it as some sort of brave escapade. However, I choose to see similarities between his path and my current quest. Greg packed the courage of his convictions and set out on a journey to merge adventure and inquiry, the goal being to immerse himself in the moment. I like to think that's the route I've taken, too.

When I parked Covfefe this morning, there were only a handful of cars in the lot. By the time I return in mid-afternoon, there are hundreds. I roam through the rows and spot license plates from Arizona, California, Texas, Utah, Florida, Washington, Missouri, New Mexico, North Carolina, South Carolina, Ohio, Oregon, Michigan, Wisconsin, Kansas, Iowa, Virginia, Tennessee, Alabama, Minnesota, Colorado, Kentucky, Oklahoma, Wyoming, Georgia, Rhode Island, Maryland, Nevada, New Jersey.... A blue Silverado with a "Back the Blue" window decal is parked next to a Volkswagen Jetta shouting "Bernie 2016." Parked in a disabled spot, a silver Cadillac sports an "I Support Wounded Warriors" bumper sticker. Twenty feet away sits a cream-colored VW bus bedecked in dozens of decals: "Let it Be"... "Day Tripper"... "Cannibus." A BMW motorcycle with a "The World is Flat" decal. A bright red Veloster L6T from Indiana. A personalized license plate from Nebraska: WHATEVR.

I know it's only a stretch of pavement next to a big hole, but the image counters the notion of a nation irreparably divided. There are places, it seems, where we can actually come together. I even begin to feel sensations to which I am unaccustomed as of late. What is this strangeness? A speck of sanguinity, perhaps? A touch of serenity? Almost—dare I say it?—hopefulness?

It might just be dehydration.

Sixty year ago, Steinbeck wrote, "We find after years of struggle that we do not take a trip; a trip takes us." Perhaps each of us here at this world wonder has answered a call from our subconscious to undertake a pilgrimage, to shed conflicting identities and attitudes and share a sense of awe with strangers, to be reminded by nature that the calamities of humankind are only a comparative blip in time.

And maybe this particular moment will prove to have been an overstated cause for concern. It could be that, years hence, my grandchildren will open a history book to find that the nadir of 2020 has been recast as a tipping point toward enlightenment. A nation recovered. The republic survived. America reemerged as a beacon of light and welcome. Saving the planet became a cooperative ambition. Protest and the prospect of voter suppression inspired a collective consciousness-raising. The narratives of the disenfranchised went unignored. The rule of law prevailed. Honesty, dignity, and decency returned to the White House. Bigotry, bullying, and conspiracy theories were once again relegated to dark places. Science was celebrated. Toxic masculinity was toppled. Glass ceilings were shattered. Civil discourse outmuscled civil unrest. Karma came out of hibernation.

Or maybe not. But I do know that there is no bridge across the Grand Canyon. To cross the divide, you have to descend all the way down before you can climb back up.

The most important election in generations is nigh. The man who is supposed to be the president of the United States is preparing to undermine democracy one last, terrifying time. Tensions are simmering. COVID is surging. And Covfefe is sputtering. There are another 700 miles—much of it on fire—between this desert chasm and the comforts of home.

I hope we make it.